国家社科基金重大项目"美国国会涉华法案文本整理、翻译与研究（1979-2019）"阶段性成果(项目编号:19ZDA168)

美国合同法重述

第二版·规则部分

Restatement of the Law
Second, Contracts

美国法学会 ◎ 编写

徐文彬 ◎ 译　　张法连 ◎ 译审

中国政法大学出版社

2022·北京

美国合同法重述第二版·规则部分

Restatement of the Law Second, Contracts copyright © 1981 by The American Law Institute (Philadelphia, Pennsylvania, U. S. A.). The American Law Institute has authorized the reproduction and translation contained in this publication, however, it has not reviewed or approved the translation and China University of Political Science and Law Press Co. , Ltd. bears the sole responsibility for the accuracy of the translation. All rights are reserved. For any additional requests to duplicate ALI material, please visit The American Law Institute website at www. ali. org. The original work in English contains extensive Comments and Reporter's Notes not included in this publication.

本书英文原版由美国法学会出版，中文版经其授权翻译出版。中国政法大学出版社对译文的准确性负责。版权所有，侵权必究。如需复制美国法学会作品，请访问其网站：www. ali. org。中文版不包含英文原版中的"评论"与"重述注释"等内容。

TABLE OF CONTENTS
目　录

第一章

术语含义

Chapter 1

MEANING OF TERMS

§ 1. Contract Defined

A contract is a promise or a set of promises for the breach of which the law gives a remedy, or the performance of which the law in some way recognizes as a duty.

第 1 条 合同

合同，是指违反之法律则给予救济，或者其履行法律以某种方式视为义务的允诺或者允诺组合。[1]

§ 2. Promise; Promisor; Promisee; Beneficiary

(1) A promise is a manifestation of intention to act or refrain from acting in a specified way, so made as to justify a promisee in understanding that a commitment has been made.

(2) The person manifesting the intention is the promisor.

(3) The person to whom the manifestation is addressed is the promisee.

(4) Where performance will benefit a person other than the promisee, that person is beneficiary.

第 2 条 允诺；允诺人；受诺人；受益人

(1) 允诺，是指以特定方式行为或者不以特定方式行为[2]的意思表

---

〔1〕 本定义的其他译法有："合同是一项或者一组这样的诺言；它或它们一旦被违反，法律就会给予救济；或者是法律以某种方式确认的义务的履行"（王军 1996：1）；"契约乃为一个允诺或一组之允诺。违反此一允诺时，法律给予救济；或其对允诺之履行，法律在某些情况下视为一项义务"（杨桢 2000：1）。两位教授的译法明白易懂，供大家参考。译者在此尝试使用一句话译出，目的是保存原句逻辑关系，同时方便记忆与传播：全句的主干结构是"合同，是指……的允诺或者允诺组合"，"允诺或者允诺组合"前面的定语较长，其逻辑层次可用分隔号表示为：违反之 ‖ 法律则给予救济，或者其履行 ‖ 法律以某种方式视为义务。

〔2〕 以特定方式行为或者不以特定方式行为（act or refrain from acting in a specified way），法律汉语中的行为一般包括积极的作为与消极的不作为，此处即涵盖了"作为"与"不作为"两种形式，但若译为"以特定方式作为或者不作为"，似乎与原意稍有不同，故作此译。另外，为了确保意义忠实并保持同一术语同一译名，本书没有使用"作为"与"不作为"这一组术语，而代之以"行为"与"不行为"。

示，且表示方式足以使受诺人合理地认为允诺人作出了郑重其事的许诺。

（2）作出意思表示的人是允诺人。

（3）意思表示指向的对象是受诺人。

（4）履行使受诺人之外的人获利的，获利人是受益人。

§ 3. Agreement Defined; Bargain Defined

An agreement is a manifestation of mutual assent on the part of two or more persons. A bargain is an agreement to exchange promises or to exchange a promise for a performance or to exchange performances.

第 3 条　协议的定义；交易的定义[1]

协议，是指两个或者两个以上的人相互同意的表示。交易，是指相互交换允诺、用允诺交换履行或者相互交换履行的协议。

§ 4. How a Promise May Be Made

A promise may be stated in words either oral or written, or may be inferred wholly or partly from conduct.

第 4 条　允诺的表达方式

允诺可以使用口头或者书面语词表达，也可以全部或者部分根据行为推断。

§ 5. Terms of Promise, Agreement, or Contract

（1）A term of a promise or agreement is that portion of the intention or assent manifested which relates to a particular matter.

（2）A term of a contract is that portion of the legal relations resulting from the

---

[1] 根据 Garner（2009）的解释以及《美国合同法重述》（下文简称"重述"）的上下文，agreement, bargain, contract 三词内涵由宽及窄，文中分别译为"协议""交易""合同"。参见 Garner, Bryan A.: Black's Law Dictionary, Thomson Reuters, 2009。由于缺乏合适的译名，下文的 transaction 也译为"交易"，但根据语境可以分辨出后者指具体的交易，而本条的"交易"（bargain）是更抽象的概念。

promise or a set of promises which relates to a particular matter, whether or not the parties manifest an intention to create those relations.

第 5 条　允诺、协议或者合同的条款

（1）允诺或者协议的条款，是指意思表示或者同意表示中与特定事项相联系的部分。

（2）合同的条款，是指允诺或者允诺组合产生的法律关系中与特定事项相联系的部分，无论当事人是否具有创设该法律关系的意思表示。

§ 6. Formal Contracts

The following types of contracts are subject in some respects to special rules that depend on their formal characteristics and differ from those governing contracts in general:

(a) Contracts under seal,

(b) Recognizances,

(c) Negotiable instruments and documents,

(d) Letters of credit.

第 6 条　要式合同

下列类型的合同在有些方面须遵守取决于其形式特征的、不同于一般合同规则的特殊规则：

(a) 盖印合同，

(b) 具结,[1]

(c) 流通票据与单据，

(d) 信用证。

---

〔1〕具结（recognizance），薛波（2003）将其译为"具结""保证"，指"在存卷法院或在经授权的治安法官（magistrate）前作出的保证"，"具结人保证实施某项行为，如按时到庭、遵纪守法、清偿债款、支付费用等"。此解释与"重述"原文的本条评论部分相似。

§ 7. Voidable Contracts

A voidable contract is one where one or more parties have the power, by a manifestation of election to do so, to avoid the legal relations created by the contract, or by ratification of the contract to extinguish the power of avoidance.

第 7 条　可撤销合同

可撤销合同，是指一个或者一个以上的当事人有权通过作出选择表示以撤销合同创设的法律关系，或者通过追认合同使撤销权归于消灭的合同。

§ 8. Unenforceable Contracts

An unenforceable contract is one for the breach of which neither the remedy of damages nor the remedy of specific performance is available, but which is recognized in some other way as creating a duty of performance, though there has been no ratification.

第 8 条　不可强制执行合同

不可强制执行合同，是指违约发生时既不产生损害赔偿金救济，也不产生具体履行〔1〕救济，但即使尚未被追认，也在其他方面被认为创设了履行义务的合同。

---

〔1〕 具体履行（specific performance），该术语也译为“强制履行”“实际履行”等，前译参见杨桢：《英美契约法论》，北京大学出版社 2000 年版。后译参见王军：《美国合同法》，中国政法大学出版社 1996 年版。

第二章
合同的成立
——当事人与行为能力[1]

◆

Chapter 2
FORMATION OF CONTRACTS
——PARTIES AND CAPACITY

---

[1] 行为能力（capacity），capacity在通用英语和法律英语中都是多义词，在法律英语中的含义也因法律部门不同而异，在民商法中也不完全对应"行为能力"，所以译者并没有将该词译名进行同一化处理，而是依靠搭配与上下文界定其含义，请读者阅读时结合语境理解。capacity的反义词incapacity与此类似。

§ 9. Parties Required

There must be at least two parties to a contract, a promisor and a promisee, but there may be any greater number.

第 9 条　当事人要求

合同至少需要两方当事人，即允诺人和受诺人，但是可以更多。

§ 10. Multiple Promisors and Promisees of the Same Performance

(1) Where there are more promisors than one in a contract, some or all of them may promise the same performance, whether or not there are also promises for separate performances.

(2) Where there are more promisees than one in a contract, a promise may be made to some or all of them as a unit, whether or not the same or another performance is separately promised to one or more of them.

第 10 条　同一履行有数个允诺人、受诺人

(1) 合同的允诺人超过一个的，部分或者所有允诺人可以允诺同一履行，无论是否也允诺了单独的履行。

(2) 合同的受诺人超过一个的，可以将部分或者所有受诺人视为整体而作出允诺，无论是否向其中一人或者一人以上单独允诺了同一履行或者其他履行。

§ 11. When a Person May Be Both Promisor and Promisee

A contract may be formed between two or more persons acting as a unit and one or more but fewer than all of these persons, acting either singly or with other persons.

第 11 条　何时允诺人与受诺人可以同为一人

合同可以在两人或者两人以上形成的整体与整体中的一人或者一人以上

但少于总数的人之间订立，后者可以单独行为，也可以协同他人行为。

§ 12. Capacity to Contract

（1）No one can be bound by contract who has not legal capacity to incur at least voidable contractual duties. Capacity to contract may be partial and its existence in respect of a particular transaction may depend upon the nature of the transaction or upon other circumstances.

（2）A natural person who manifests assent to a transaction has full legal capacity to incur contractual duties thereby unless he is

（a）under guardianship, or

（b）an infant, or

（c）mentally ill or defective, or

（d）intoxicated.

第 12 条　缔约能力

（1）凡不具备承担至少是可撤销合同义务的法定能力的，不受合同约束。缔约能力可以部分具备，在具体交易中是否存在可能取决于交易性质或者其他情形。

（2）除下列情形[1]以外，对交易作出同意表示的自然人具备承担由此产生的合同义务的完全法定能力：

（a）处于被监护之中的，或者

（b）是未成年人的，或者

（c）有精神疾患或者缺陷的，或者

（d）处于麻醉状态的。

---

〔1〕 下列情形，汉语立法文本中往往通过"下列情形"或者"下列情形之一"来区分叠加性或者选择性的情形，但为了兼顾表述与忠实，译文统一使用"下列情形"，列举事项的叠加或者选择通过各项后面的"或者""且"等字眼并结合语境进行区分。

§ 13. Persons Affected by Guardianship

A person has no capacity to incur contractual duties if his property is under guardianship by reason of an adjudication of mental illness or defect.

第13条　受监护影响的人

因被判定有精神疾患或者缺陷而财产处于监护中的人，不具备承担合同义务的能力。

§ 14. Infants

Unless a statute provides otherwise, a natural person has the capacity to incur only voidable contractual duties until the beginning of the day before the person's eighteenth birthday.

第14条　未成年人

除制定法另有规定以外，自然人在年满18周岁生日之前的一天开始之前，只具有承担可撤销合同义务的行为能力。

§ 15. Mental Illness or Defect

（1）A person incurs only voidable contractual duties by entering into a transaction if by reason of mental illness or defect

（a）he is unable to understand in a reasonable manner the nature and consequences of the transaction, or

（b）he is unable to act in a reasonable manner in relation to the transaction and the other party has reason to know of his condition.

（2）Where the contract is made on fair terms and the other party is without knowledge of the mental illness or defect, the power of avoidance under Subsection（1）terminates to the extent that the contract has been so preformed in whole or in part or the circumstances have so changed that avoidance would be unjust. In such a case a court may grant relief as justice requires.

第 15 条　精神疾患或者缺陷

（1）由于精神疾患或者缺陷而有下列情形的人，缔结交易后只承担可撤销合同义务：

（a）不能合理地理解交易性质及其后果的，或者

（b）不能以合理的方式从事与交易有关的行为，且对方有理由知道的。

（2）订立的合同条款公平，且对方不知道缔约人的精神疾患或者缺陷的，在合同已经全部或者部分履行，或者情形已经发生改变，因而撤销合同会有失公正的范围内，第（1）款规定的撤销权终止。在此情况下，法院可以根据公正所需判予救济。

§ 16. Intoxicated Persons

A person incurs only voidable contractual duties by entering into a transaction if the other party has reason to know that by reason of intoxication

（a）he is unable to understand in a reasonable manner the nature and consequences of the transaction, or

（b）he is unable to act in a reasonable manner in relation to the transaction.

第 16 条　处于麻醉状态的人

由于处于麻醉状态而有下列情形且对方有理由知道的，处于麻醉状态的人缔结交易后只承担可撤销合同的义务：

（a）不能合理地理解交易性质及其后果的，或者

（b）不能以合理的方式从事与交易有关的行为的。

第三章

合同的成立
——相互同意

Chapter 3

FORMATION OF CONTRACTS
——MUTUAL ASSENT

TOPIC 1. IN GENERAL
第一节 一般规则

§ 17. Requirement of a Bargain

(1) Except as stated in Subsection (2), the formation of a contract requires a bargain in which there is a manifestation of mutual assent to the exchange and a consideration.

(2) Whether or not there is a bargain a contract may be formed under special rules applicable to formal contracts or under the rules stated in §§ 82-94.

第 17 条 交易要求

(1) 除第 (2) 款所述规则以外，合同成立必须存在交易，即当事人对交换表示相互同意并存在对价。

(2) 无论是否存在交易，适用要式合同的特殊规则或者第 82~94 条所述规则有规定的，合同仍然可以成立。

TOPIC 2. MANIFESTATION OF ASSENT IN GENERAL
第二节 同意表示的一般规则

§ 18. Manifestation of Mutual Assent

Manifestation of mutual assent to an exchange requires that each party either make a promise or begin or render a performance.

第 18 条 相互同意的表示

对交换作出相互同意的表示，要求各方当事人或者作出允诺，或者开始履行或给付履行。

§ 19. Conduct as Manifestation of Assent

(1) The manifestation of assent may be made wholly or partly by written or spoken words or by other acts or by failure to act.

(2) The conduct of a party is not effective as a manifestation of his assent unless he intends to engage in the conduct and knows or has reason to know that the other party may infer from his conduct that he assents.

(3) The conduct of a party may manifest assent even though he does not in fact assent. In such cases a resulting contract may be voidable because of fraud, duress, mistake, or other invalidation cause.

第 19 条　行为作为同意表示

(1) 同意表示可以全部或者部分通过书面或者口头语词作出，也可以通过其他行为或者不行为作出。

(2) 只有当事人具有从事行为的意图，且知道或者有理由知道对方可以从其行为中推测出其已同意时，当事人的行为才是有效的同意表示。

(3) 即使没有事实上的同意，当事人的行为也可以构成同意表示。在此情况下，产生的合同可能因欺诈、胁迫、错误或者其他无效事由而成为可撤销合同。

§ 20. Effect of Misunderstanding

(1) There is no manifestation of mutual assent to an exchange if the parties attach materially different meanings to their manifestations and

(a) neither party knows or has reason to know the meaning attached by the other; or

(b) each party knows or each party has reason to know the meaning attached by the other.

(2) The manifestations of the parties are operative in accordance with the meaning attached to them by one of the parties if

（a）that party does not know of any different meaning attached by the other, and the other knows the meaning attached by the first party; or

（b）that party has no reason to know of any different meaning attached by the other, and the other has reason to know the meaning attached by the first party.

第 20 条　误解的效力

（1）当事人对各自的表示赋予了实质上不同的含义并且有下列情形的，不存在对交换的相互同意表示：

（a）任何一方都不知道或者没有理由知道对方所赋予的含义的；或者

（b）各方当事人知道或者各方当事人有理由知道对方所赋予的含义的。

（2）一方当事人有下列情形的，各方当事人的表示以该方当事人赋予的含义为准：

（a）该方当事人不知道对方赋予了不同含义，而对方知道该方当事人所赋予的含义的；或者

（b）该方当事人没有理由知道对方赋予了不同含义，而对方有理由知道该方当事人赋予的含义的。

§ 21. Intention to Be Legally Bound

Neither real nor apparent intention that a promise be legally binding is essential to the formation of a contract, but a manifestation of intention that a promise shall not affect legal relations may prevent the formation of a contract.

第 21 条　受法律约束的意思表示

允诺具有法律约束力的意思表示，无论真实的还是表见的，都不是合同成立所必需，但允诺不影响法律关系的意思表示则可以阻却合同的成立。

§ 22. Mode of Assent: Offer and Acceptance

（1）The manifestation of mutual assent to an exchange ordinarily takes the form of an offer or proposal by one party followed by an acceptance by the other party or parties.

（2）A manifestation of mutual assent may be made even though neither offer nor acceptance can be identified and even though the moment of formation cannot be determined.

第 22 条　同意的方式：要约与承诺

（1）对交换表示相互同意的，一般采取一方提出要约或者提议，对方或者其他各方随后进行承诺的形式。

（2）即使既不能辨识要约，也不能辨识承诺，甚至也不能确定成立时刻，也可能作出了相互同意的表示。

§ 23. Necessity That Manifestation Have Reference to Each Other

It is essential to a bargain that each party manifest assent with reference to the manifestation of the other.

第 23 条　表示相互参指的必要性

若要构成交易，每一方当事人的同意表示必须针对对方的表示作出。

TOPIC 3. MAKING OF OFFERS
第三节　要约的作出

§ 24. Offer Defined

An offer is the manifestation of willingness to enter into a bargain, so made as to justify another person in understanding that his assent to that bargain is invited and will conclude it.

第 24 条　要约的定义

要约，是指进行交易的意愿表示，且表示方式使得他人合理地认为，自己受到了作出同意表示的邀请，且一经同意即可达成交易。

§ 25. Option Contracts

An option contract is a promise which meets the requirements for the formation of a contract and limits the promisor's power to revoke an offer.

第 25 条 选择权合同

选择权合同，是指符合合同成立要求但限制了允诺人撤销要约权利的允诺。

§ 26. Preliminary Negotiations

A manifestation of willingness to enter into a bargain is not an offer if the person to whom it is addressed knows or has reason to know that the person making it does not intend to conclude a bargain until he has made a further manifestation of assent.

第 26 条 初步磋商

相对人知道或者有理由知道，交易意愿表示人在作出进一步同意表示之前没有达成交易的意图的，交易意愿表示不是要约。

§ 27. Existence of Contract Where Written Memorial is Contemplated

Manifestations of assent that are in themselves sufficient to conclude a contract will not be prevented from so operating by the fact that the parties also manifest an intention to prepare and adopt a written memorial thereof; but the circumstances may show that the agreements are preliminary negotiations.

第 27 条 考虑制作书面备忘录时合同的存在

各方的同意表示本身足以缔结合同的，不因当事人也作出制作、采用书面备忘录的意思表示而受阻却；但情形可能表明，达成的协议仅是初步磋商。

§ 28. Auctions

(1) At an auction, unless a contrary intention is manifested,

(a) the auctioneer invites offers from successive bidders which he may accept or reject;

(b) when goods are put up without reserve, the auctioneer makes an offer to sell at any price bid by the highest bidder, and after the auctioneer calls for bids the goods cannot be withdrawn unless no bid is made within a reasonable time;

(c) whether or not the auction is without reserve, a bidder may withdraw his bid until the auctioneer's announcement of completion of the sale, but a bidder's retraction does not revive any previous bid.

(2) Unless a contrary intention is manifested, bids at an auction embody terms made known by advertisement, posting or other publication of which bidders are or should be aware, as modified by any announcement made by the auctioneer when the goods are put up.

第 28 条 拍卖

(1) 除有相反意思表示的以外，在拍卖场合：

(a) 拍卖人邀请竞拍人相继发出要约，可以接受，也可以拒绝；

(b) 放置拍卖物进行无底价拍卖时，拍卖人即发出按照出价最高者所提出的任何价格出售拍卖物的要约，且拍卖人请求出价之后，除合理时间内无人出价的以外，拍卖物不得撤回；

(c) 无论是否保留底价，竞拍人在拍卖人宣布成交之前可以撤回出价，但撤回出价并不导致先前出价生效。

(2) 除有相反意思表示的以外，拍卖中的出价体现广告、招贴或者其他出版物公开的竞拍人知晓或者应当知晓的条款，包括拍卖物进入竞拍时拍卖人公告中的任何变更。

§ 29. To Whom an Offer is Addressed

(1) The manifested intention of the offeror determines the person or persons in whom is created a power of acceptance.

(2) An offer may create a power of acceptance in a specified person or in one or more of a specified group or class of persons, acting separately or together, or in any-one or everyone who makes a specified promise or renders a specified performance.

第 29 条　要约向谁发出

(1) 要约人的意思表示决定有承诺权力的人。

(2) 要约确定的有承诺权力的人，可以是指定的人，也可以是指定团体或者类别中的一个或者一个以上的单独行动或者集体行动的人，还可以是作出指定允诺或者给付指定履行的任何人或者所有人。

§ 30. Form of Acceptance Invited

(1) An offer may invite or require acceptance to be made by an affirmative an-swer in words, or by performing or refraining from performing a specified act, or may empower the offeree to make a selection of terms in his acceptance.

(2) Unless otherwise indicated by the language or the circumstances, an offer invites acceptance in any manner and by any medium reasonable in the circum-stances.

第 30 条　请求的承诺形式

(1) 要约可以请求或者要求通过使用语词作出肯定性答复，或者作出或不作出特定行为进行承诺，也可以授权受要约人在承诺中进行条款选择。

(2) 除语言或者情形另有所示以外，要约请求采用具体情形下的任何合理方式、合理媒介进行承诺。

§ 31. Offer Proposing a Single Contract or a Number of Contracts

An offer may propose the formation of a single contract by a single acceptance or the formation of a number of contracts by successive acceptances from time to time.

第 31 条　要约提议缔结单个合同或者数个合同

要约可以提议通过一次性承诺成立单个合同，或者通过先后阶段性承诺成立数个合同。

§ 32. Invitation of Promise or Performance

In case of doubt an offer is interpreted as inviting the offeree to accept either by promising to perform what the offer requests or by rendering the performance, as the offeree chooses.

第 32 条　请求允诺或者履行

存在疑问时，要约解释为请求受诺人既可以通过允诺要约要求的履行进行承诺，也可以通过给付该履行进行承诺，由受要约人自行选择。

§ 33. Certainty

（1）Even though a manifestation of intention is intended to be understood as an offer, it cannot be accepted so as to form a contract unless the terms of the contract are reasonably certain.

（2）The terms of a contract are reasonably certain if they provide a basis for determining the existence of a breach and for giving an appropriate remedy.

（3）The fact that one or more terms of a proposed bargain are left open or uncertain may show that a manifestation of intention is not intended to be understood as an offer or as an acceptance.

第 33 条　确定性

（1）即使意思表示希望被视为要约，但是只有合同条款具备合理确定性时，方可被承诺进而成立合同。

（2）合同条款提供了判断违约存在和给予适当救济的基础的，条款具备合理的确定性。

（3）所提议交易中有一个或者多个条款是开放性或者不确定的，可能表明意思表示并不希望被理解为要约或者承诺。

§ 34. Certainty and Choice of Terms; Effect of Performance or Reliance

（1）The terms of a contract may be reasonably certain even though it empowers one or both parties to make a selection of terms in the course of performance.

（2）Part performance under an agreement may remove uncertainty and establish that a contract enforceable as a bargain has been formed.

（3）Action in reliance on an agreement may make a contractual remedy appropriate even though uncertainty is not removed.

第 34 条 条款确定性与条款选择；履行或者信赖的效力

（1）即使合同授权一方或者双方当事人在履行过程中选择条款，合同条款仍然可能具备合理的确定性。

（2）协议项下的部分履行可以消除不确定性，并证明作为交易的可强制执行合同已经成立。

（3）即使不确定性没有消除，因信赖协议而采取的行为也可以使某个合同救济变得适当。

TOPIC 4. DURATION OF THE OFFEREE'S POWER OF ACCEPTANCE
第四节 受要约人承诺权的期间

§ 35. The Offeree's Power of Acceptance

（1）An offer gives to the offeree a continuing power to complete the manifestation of mutual assent by acceptance of the offer.

（2）A contract cannot be created by acceptance of an offer after the power of acceptance has been terminated in one of the ways listed in §36.

第 35 条　受要约人的承诺权

（1）要约赋予受要约人通过对要约进行承诺以完成相互同意表示的持续权利。

（2）承诺权按照第 36 条列举的方式之一被终止后，对要约进行承诺不能成立合同。

§36. Methods of Termination of the Power of Acceptance

（1）An offeree's power of acceptance may be terminated by

（a）rejection or counter-offer by the offeree, or

（b）lapse of time, or

（c）revocation by the offeror, or

（d）death or incapacity of the offeror or offeree.

（2）In addition, an offeree's power of acceptance is terminated by the non-occurrence of any condition of acceptance under the terms of the offer.

第 36 条　终止承诺权的方法

（1）受要约人的承诺权可以因下列事由而终止：

（a）受要约人拒绝要约或者作出反要约，或者

（b）期间届满，或者

（c）要约人撤销要约，或者

（d）要约人或者受要约人死亡或者丧失行为能力。

（2）此外，要约条款规定的任何承诺条件没有成就的，受要约人的承诺权终止。

§37. Termination of Power of Acceptance Under Option Contract

Not withstanding §§38-49, the power of acceptance under an option contract is not terminated by rejection or counter-offer, by revocation, or by death or incapacity of the offeror, unless the requirements are met for the discharge of a contractual duty.

第 37 条 选择权合同项下的承诺权终止

虽然第 38~49 条有规定，但除满足解除合同义务要求的以外，选择权合同规定的承诺权并不因拒绝或反要约，撤销，或者要约人死亡或丧失行为能力而终止。

§ 38. Rejection

(1) An offeree's power of acceptance is terminated by his rejection of the offer, unless the offeror has manifested a contrary intention.

(2) A manifestation of intention not to accept an offer is a rejection unless the offeree manifests an intention to take it under further advisement.

第 38 条 拒绝

(1) 受要约人的承诺权因拒绝要约而终止，但要约人作出相反意思表示的除外。

(2) 对要约不予承诺的意思表示是拒绝，但受要约人表示还要进一步考虑的除外。

§ 39. Counter-offers

(1) A counter-offer is an offer made by an offeree to his offeror relating to the same matter as the original offer and proposing a substituted bargain differing from that proposed by the original offer.

(2) An offeree's power of acceptance is terminated by his making of a counter-offer, unless the offeror has manifested a contrary intention or unless the counter-offer manifests a contrary intention of the offeree.

第 39 条 反要约

(1) 反要约，是指受要约人向要约人就相同事项作出的、提出与原始要约不同的替代交易的要约。

（2）受要约人的承诺权因作出反要约而终止，但要约人作出相反意思表示，或者反要约表示了受要约人相反意思表示的除外。

§ 40. Time When Rejection or Counter-offer Terminates the Power of Acceptance

Rejection or counter-offer by mail or telegram does not terminate the power of acceptance until received by the offeror, but limits the power so that a letter or telegram of acceptance started after the sending of an otherwise effective rejection or counter-offer is only a counter-offer unless the acceptance is received by the offeror before he receives the rejection or counter-offer.

第 40 条　拒绝或者反要约终止承诺权的时间

通过邮件或者电报作出的拒绝或者反要约，在要约人收到之前并不终止承诺权，而是构成对承诺权的限制，因而发出在其他方面都有效的拒绝或者反要约之后，重新发送的承诺函或者承诺电报仅为反要约，但要约人在收到拒绝或者反要约之前收到承诺的除外。

§ 41. Lapse of Time

(1) An offeree's power of acceptance is terminated at the time specified in the offer, or, if no time is specified, at the end of a reasonable time.

(2) What is a reasonable time is a question of fact, depending on all the circumstances existing when the offer and attempted acceptance are made.

(3) Unless otherwise indicated by the language or the circumstances, and subject to the rule stated in §49, an offer sent by mail is seasonably accepted if an acceptance is mailed at any time before midnight on the day on which the offer is received.

第 41 条　期间届满

（1）受要约人的承诺权在要约规定的时间终止；要约没有规定终止时间的，在合理的时间结束后终止。

（2）何为合理时间是事实问题，取决于要约和试图承诺作出时存在的所有情形。

（3）除非语言或者情形另有所示，在符合第49条所述规则的前提下，在要约收到之日的午夜之前任何时候发出承诺邮件的，是对邮件发送的要约的及时承诺。

§ 42. Revocation by Communication from Offeror Received by Offeree

An offeree's power of acceptance is terminated when the offeree receives from the offeror a manifestation of an intention not to enter into the proposed contract.

第42条　受要约人收到要约人的撤销通知

受要约人收到要约人不缔结所提议合同的意思表示时，受要约人的承诺权终止。

§ 43. Indirect Communication of Revocation

An offeree's power of acceptance is terminated when the offeror takes definite action inconsistent with an intention to enter into the proposed contract and the offeree acquires reliable information to that effect.

第43条　撤销的间接通知

要约人采取了与缔结提议合同的意思不一致的确定行为，且受要约人获得了以此为内容的可靠信息时，受要约人的承诺权终止。

§ 44. Effect of Deposit on Revocability of Offer

An offeror's power of revocation is not limited by the deposit of money or other property to be forfeited in the event of revocation, but the deposit may be forfeited to the extent that it is not a penalty.

第44条　定金对要约可撤销性的效力

交付了金钱或者其他财产作为定金，并约定撤销要约则予以没收的，不构成对要约人撤销权的限制，但定金可以在不构成惩罚的范围内被没收。

§ 45. Option Contract Created by Part Performance or Tender

（1）Where an offer invites an offeree to accept by rendering a performance and does not invite a promissory acceptance, an option contract is created when the offeree tenders or begins the invited performance or tenders a beginning of it.

（2）The offeror's duty of performance under any option contract so created is conditional on completion or tender of the invited performance in accordance with the terms of the offer.

第 45 条　因部分履行或者提交履行〔1〕成立选择权合同

（1）要约请求受要约人以给付履行的形式作出承诺，而没有请求以允诺形式承诺的，受要约人提交或者开始受邀履行，或者提交初步履行时，成立选择权合同。

（2）如此成立的选择权合同项下要约人的履行义务，以完成或者提交符合要约条款的受邀履行为条件。

§ 46. Revocation of General Offer

Where an offer is made by advertisement in a newspaper or other general notification to the public or to a number of persons whose identity is unknown to the offeror, the offeree's power of acceptance is terminated when a notice of termination is given publicity by advertisement or other general notification equal to that given to the offer and no better means of notification is reasonably available.

---

〔1〕 提交履行（tender），以 Black's Law Dictionary 的解释为基础，tender 在本语境中的可能含义为"充分有效地提出履行，尤其是以清偿债务或者义务为目的提供金钱或者履行"（a valid and sufficient offer of performance；specif., an unconditional offer of money or performance to satisfy a debt or obligation）；如果相对人没有合理理由而拒绝接受时，提交人不会因为不予偿付或者不予履行而受到惩罚，而相对人则可能要承担违约责任。有关的搭配包括 tender of deliver, tender of performance 等。本词在合同法中的另一常用含义是"未果履行"（attempted performance），即提交人提交履行，对方拒绝接受，因而履行未能完成的情况，但本书并未出现此种意义的用法。详见 Garner（2009：1606）。与"tender"（提交、提交履行）相对照，"render"在本书中译为"给付"。

第46条　普遍要约的撤销

以在报纸上发布广告或者其他普遍性通知的形式，向公众或者不知身份的数人发出要约的，如果终止承诺权的通知也通过广告或者其他普遍性通知的形式发布，达到了与要约相同的宣传程度，且无法合理地获取更好的通知方式，受要约人的承诺权终止。

§ 47. Revocation of Divisible Offer

An offer contemplating a series of independent contracts by separate acceptances may be effectively revoked so as to terminate the power to create future contracts, though one or more of the proposed contracts have already been formed by the offeree's acceptance.

第47条　可分要约的撤销

要约通过单独承诺成立系列独立合同的，即使受要约人的承诺已经成立一个或者一个以上的所提议合同，也可以为终止创设后续合同的权力而有效撤销。

§ 48. Death or Incapacity of Offeror or Offeree

An offeree's power of acceptance is terminated when the offeree or offeror dies or is deprived of legal capacity to enter into the proposed contract.

第48条　要约人或者受要约人死亡或者丧失行为能力

受要约人或者要约人死亡，或者被剥夺缔结所提议合同的法定行为能力的，受要约人的承诺权终止。

§ 49. Effect of Delay in Communication of Offer

If communication of an offer to the offeree is delayed, the period within which a contract can be created by acceptance is not thereby extended if the offeree knows or has reason to know of the delay, though it is due to the fault of the offeror; but if the delay is due to the fault of the offeror or to the means of transmission adopted by him, and the offeree neither knows nor has reason to know that there has been delay, a contract can be created by acceptance within the period which would have been permissible if the offer had been dispatched at the time that its arrival seems to indicate.

第49条 要约传递延迟的效力

发送给受要约人的要约传递延迟的，如果受要约人知道或者有理由知道此延迟，则作出承诺创设合同的期间并不因此而延展，即使延迟是要约人过错所致；但延迟是要约人过错所致，或者是要约人采取的传输方式所致，且受要约人不知道、也没有理由知道延迟发生的，根据要约实际到达的时间推定要约发送的时间后，进而确定的承诺期间允许承诺时，作出承诺则可以创设合同。

TOPIC 5. ACCEPTANCE OF OFFERS
第五节 对要约的承诺

§ 50. Acceptance of Offer Defined; Acceptance by Performance; Acceptance by Promise

(1) Acceptance of an offer is a manifestation of assent to the terms thereof made by the offeree in a manner invited or required by the offer.

(2) Acceptance by performance requires that at least part of what the offer requests be performed or tendered and includes acceptance by a performance which operates as a return promise.

(3) Acceptance by a promise requires that the offeree complete every act essential to the making of the promise.

第50条 对要约承诺的定义；通过履行承诺；通过允诺承诺

(1) 对要约的承诺，是指受要约人依照要约所请求或者要求的方式对要约条款作出的同意表示。

（2）通过履行承诺，要求要约请求的事项至少部分得以履行或者提交，包括通过同时也是回报允诺的履行进行承诺。

（3）通过允诺承诺，要求受要约人完成作出允诺所需的所有基本行为。

§ 51. Effect of Part Performance Without Knowledge of Offer

Unless the offeror manifests a contrary intention, an offeree who learns of an offer after he has rendered part of the performance requested by the offer may accept by completing the requested performance.

第 51 条　不知道要约而部分履行的效力

除要约人作出相反意思表示的以外，受要约人给付了要约所要求的部分履行之后才得知要约存在的，可以通过完成所要求的履行进行承诺。

§ 52. Who May Accept an Offer

An offer can be accepted only by a person whom it invites to furnish the consideration.

第 52 条　谁可以对要约承诺

只有要约请求提供对价的人可以对要约承诺。

§ 53. Acceptance by Performance; Manifestation of Intention Not to Accept

（1）An offer can be accepted by the rendering of a performance only if the offer invites such an acceptance.

（2）Except as stated in §69, the rendering of a performance does not constitute an acceptance if within a reasonable time the offeree exercises reasonable diligence to notify the offeror of non-acceptance.

（3）Where an offer of a promise invites acceptance by performance and does not invite a promissory acceptance, the rendering of the invited performance does not constitute an acceptance if before the offeror performs his promise the offeree manifests an intention not to accept.

第 53 条　通过履行承诺；不予承诺的意思表示

（1）只有要约请求通过给付履行进行承诺的，才可以通过给付履行对要约承诺。

（2）除第 69 条所述规则以外，受要约人在合理时间内通过合理努力通知要约人不予承诺的，给付履行不构成承诺。

（3）允诺形式的要约请求通过履行承诺而没有请求通过允诺承诺的，如果在要约人履行允诺之前受要约人作出不予承诺的意思表示，则给付受邀履行不构成承诺。

§54. Acceptance by Performance; Necessity of Notification to Offeror

（1）Where an offer invites an offeree to accept by rendering a performance, no notification is necessary to make such an acceptance effective unless the offer requests such a notification.

（2）If an offeree who accepts by rendering a performance has reason to know that the offeror has no adequate means of learning of the performance with reasonable promptness and certainty, the contractual duty of the offeror is discharged unless

（a）the offeree exercises reasonable diligence to notify the offeror of acceptance, or

（b）the offeror learns of the performance within a reasonable time, or

（c）the offer indicates that notification of acceptance is not required.

第 54 条　通过履行承诺；通知要约人的必要性

（1）要约请求受要约人通过给付履行进行承诺的，除要约有通知要求的以外，无需作出通知承诺即可生效。

（2）除下列情形以外，通过给付履行进行承诺的受要约人，有理由知道要约人没有充分渠道以合理的速度和确定性知晓该履行的，要约人的合同义务解除：

（a）受要约人通过合理努力将承诺之事通知要约人的，或者

（b）要约人在合理时间内知晓履行的，或者

（c）要约表明不需要作出承诺通知的。

§ 55. Acceptance of Non-Promissory Offers

Acceptance by promise may create a contract in which the offeror's performance is completed when the offeree's promise is made.

第 55 条 对非允诺要约的承诺

通过允诺承诺创设的合同，可以是受要约人作出允诺时要约人已经履行完毕的合同。

§ 56. Acceptance by Promise; Necessity of Notification to Offeror

Except as stated in § 69 or where the offer manifests a contrary intention, it is essential to an acceptance by promise either that the offeree exercise reasonable diligence to notify the offeror of acceptance or that the offeror receive the acceptance seasonably.

第 56 条 通过允诺承诺；通知要约人的必要性

除第 69 条所述规则或者要约作出相反意思表示的以外，通过允诺承诺的，受要约人必须通过合理努力通知要约人承诺之事，或者要约人必须及时收到承诺。

§ 57. Effect of Equivocal Acceptance

Where notification is essential to acceptance by promise, the offeror is not bound by an acceptance in equivocal terms unless he reasonably understands it as an acceptance.

第 57 条 模糊承诺的效力

如果通知是通过允诺承诺所必需的，则要约人不受条款模糊的承诺的约束，但要约人合理地理解为承诺的除外。

§58. Necessity of Acceptance Complying with Terms of Offer

An acceptance must comply with the requirements of the offer as to the promise to be made or the performance to be rendered.

第58条　承诺遵守要约条款的必要性

承诺必须遵守要约对于将作出的允诺或者将给付的履行的要求。

§59. Purported Acceptance Which Adds Qualifications

A reply to an offer which purports to accept it but is conditional on the offeror's assent to terms additional to or different from those offered is not an acceptance but is a counter-offer.

第59条　附加限定条件的宣称承诺

对要约的回复宣称对要约进行承诺，但是以要约人同意新增的条款或者不同于要约的条款为条件的，回复不是承诺，而是反要约。

§60. Acceptance of Offer Which States Place, Time or Manner of Acceptance

If an offer prescribes the place, time or manner of acceptance its terms in this respect must be complied with in order to create a contract. If an offer merely suggests a permitted place, time or manner of acceptance, another method of acceptance is not precluded.

第60条　对载有承诺地点、时间或者方式的要约进行承诺

要约规定了承诺的地点、时间或者方式的，必须遵守要约的此类条款才能创设合同。要约仅仅建议承诺的地点、时间或者方式的，不排除其他的承诺方法。

§ 61. Acceptance Which Requests Change of Terms

An acceptance which requests a change or addition to the terms of the offer is not thereby invalidated unless the acceptance is made to depend on an assent to the changed or added terms.

第 61 条　要求改变条款的承诺

要求改变或者增加要约条款的承诺并不因此而无效，但表明承诺与否取决于同意条款改变或者增加的除外。

§ 62. Effect of Performance by Offeree Where Offer Invites Either Performance or Promise

（1）Where an offer invites an offeree to choose between acceptance by promise and acceptance by performance, the tender or beginning of the invited performance or a tender of a beginning of it is an acceptance by performance.

（2）Such an acceptance operates as a promise to render complete performance.

第 62 条　要约请求履行或者允诺时，受要约人履行的效力

（1）要约请求受要约人在通过允诺承诺和通过履行承诺之间选择的，提交或者开始受邀履行，或者提交初步履行，是通过履行承诺。

（2）这种承诺等同于允诺给付完整履行。

§ 63. Time When Acceptance Takes Effect

Unless the offer provides otherwise,

（a）an acceptance made in a manner and by a medium invited by an offer is operative and completes the manifestation of mutual assent as soon as put out of the offeree's possession, without regard to whether it ever reaches the offeror; but

（b）an acceptance under an option contract is not operative until received by the offeror.

第 63 条　承诺生效的时间

除要约另有规定以外，

（a）按照要约要求的方式和媒介作出的承诺，一旦脱离受要约人的控制即产生效力，并完成相互同意表示，而无论是否到达要约人；但是

（b）选择权合同项下的承诺，只有要约人收到时方为生效。

§ 64. Acceptance by Telephone or Teletype

Acceptance given by telephone or other medium of substantially instantaneous two-way communication is governed by the principles applicable to acceptances where the parties are in the presence of each other.

第 64 条　通过电话或者电传承诺

通过电话或者其他实质上的即时双向传递媒介作出承诺的，适用当事人当面承诺时的原则。

§ 65. Reasonableness of Medium of Acceptance

Unless circumstances known to the offeree indicate otherwise, a medium of acceptance is reasonable if it is the one used by the offeror or one customary in similar transactions at the time and place the offer is received.

第 65 条　承诺媒介的合理性

除受要约人知道的情形另有表示以外，如果承诺的媒介是要约人所使用的，或者在要约收到的时间和地点是类似交易所惯常使用的，承诺媒介是合理媒介。

§ 66. Acceptance Must Be Properly Dispatched

An acceptance sent by mail or otherwise from a distance is not operative when dispatched, unless it is properly addressed and such other precautions taken as are ordinarily observed to insure safe transmission of similar messages.

第 66 条 承诺必须正确发出

从一定距离通过邮件或者其他方式发送的承诺，只有地址书写正确，并且采取了安全传递类似信息通常采取的其他预防措施的，才在发出之时生效。

§ 67. Effect of Receipt of Acceptance Improperly Dispatched

Where an acceptance is seasonably dispatched but the offeree uses means of transmission not invited by the offer or fails to exercise reasonable diligence to insure safe transmission, it is treated as operative upon dispatch if received within the time in which a properly dispatched acceptance would normally have arrived.

第 67 条 收到未正确发送的承诺的效力

承诺及时发出，但受要约人没有使用要约要求的传输方式，或者没有尽到合理努力以确保安全传输的，如果收到的时间处于正确发出的承诺正常到达的范围之内，则视为发出时生效。

§ 68. What Constitutes Receipt of Revocation, Rejection, or Acceptance

A written revocation, rejection, or acceptance is received when the writing comes into the possession of the person addressed, or of some person authorized by him to receive it for him, or when it is deposited in some place which he has authorized as the place for this or similar communications to be deposited for him.

第 68 条 何为收到撤销、拒绝或者承诺

撤销、拒绝或者承诺文件进入收件人，或者收件人授权的代收人控制范围之内的，或者投放于收件人授权的本件或者类似传输件存放之所的，即为收到书面撤销、拒绝或者承诺。

§ 69. Acceptance by Silence or Exercise of Dominion

(1) Where an offeree fails to reply to an offer, his silence and inaction operate as an acceptance in the following cases only:

(a) Where an offeree takes the benefit of offered services with reasonable opportunity to reject them and reason to know that they were offered with the expectation of compensation.

(b) Where the offeror has stated or given the offeree reason to understand that assent may be manifested by silence or inaction, and the offeree in remaining silent and inactive intends to accept the offer.

(c) Where because of previous dealings or otherwise, it is reasonable that the offeree should notify the offeror if he does not intend to accept.

(2) An offeree who does any act inconsistent with the offeror's ownership of offered property is bound in accordance with the offered terms unless they are manifestly unreasonable. But if the act is wrongful as against the offeror it is an acceptance only if ratified by him.

第 69 条　通过沉默或行使支配权进行承诺

（1）受要约人没有对要约作出答复的，其沉默与不行为只在下列情形下是承诺：

（a）受要约人有合理机会拒绝所提供的服务，也有理由知道服务是有偿的，但仍然接受了服务利益的。

（b）要约人已经说明或者使受要约人有理由相信，可以通过沉默或者不行为作出同意表示，并且受要约人保持沉默和不行为的意思表示就是对要约进行承诺的。

（c）由于先前交易或者其他情况，受要约人若无承诺的意思表示就应通知要约人是合理的。

（2）受要约人的行为与要约人所提供财产的所有权相矛盾的，除要约条款明显不合理的以外，受要约人受到要约条款的约束。行为是针对要约人的不法行为的，只有要约人追认后才是承诺。

§ 70. Effect of Receipt by Offeror of a Late or Otherwise Defective Acceptance

A late or otherwise defective acceptance may be effective as an offer to the original offeror, but his silence operates as an acceptance in such a case only as stated in § 69.

第 70 条　要约人收到迟到承诺或者有其他缺陷的承诺的效力

迟到的或者有其他缺陷的承诺，其效力可能是对原始要约人发出的要约，但只有在第 69 条所述情况下，原始要约人的沉默才构成承诺。

第四章
合同的成立
——对价

Chapter 4
FORMATION OF CONTRACTS
——CONSIDERATION

TOPIC 1. THE REQUIREMENT OF CONSIDERATION
第一节 对价的要求

§71. Requirement of Exchange; Types of Exchange

（1）To constitute consideration, a performance or a return promise must be bargained for.

（2）A performance or return promise is bargained for if it is sought by the promisor in exchange for his promise and is given by the promisee in exchange for that promise.

（3）The performance may consist of

（a）an act other than a promise, or

（b）a forbearance, or

（c）the creation, modification, or destruction of a legal relation.

（4）The performance or return promise may be given to the promisor or to some other person. It may be given by the promisee or by some other person.

第71条 交换要求；交换的种类

（1）若要构成对价，履行或者回报允诺必须是交易的对象。

（2）履行或者回报允诺是允诺人以自己的允诺寻求交换的对象，并由受诺人给予以交换允诺人的允诺的，即为交易的对象。

（3）履行可以包括：

（a）除允诺以外的行为，或者

（b）不行为，或者

（c）法律关系的创设、变更或者消灭。

（4）履行或者回报允诺可以给予允诺人或者其他人，也可以由受诺人或者其他人给予。

§ 72. Exchange of Promise for Performance

Except as stated in §§ 73 and 74, any performance which is bargained for is consideration.

第 72 条　以允诺交换履行

除第 73 条和第 74 条所述规则以外，作为交易对象的任何履行都是对价。

§ 73. Performance of Legal Duty

Performance of a legal duty owed to a promisor which is neither doubtful nor the subject of honest dispute is not consideration; but a similar performance is consideration if it differs from what was required by the duty in a way which reflects more than a pretense of bargain.

第 73 条　法定义务的履行

应当向允诺人履行且既无疑问又非诚实争议的法定义务，其履行不是对价；但不同于法定义务的要求，且反映的不仅仅是表面交易的类似履行是对价。

§ 74. Settlement of Claims

(1) Forbearance to assert or the surrender of a claim or defense which proves to be invalid is not consideration unless

(a) the claim or defense is in fact doubtful because of uncertainty as to the facts or the law, or

(b) the forbearing or surrendering party believes that the claim or defense may be fairly determined to be valid.

(2) The execution of a written instrument surrendering a claim or defense by one who is under no duty to execute it is consideration if the execution of the written instrument is bargained for even though he is not asserting the claim or defense and believes that no valid claim or defense exists.

第 74 条　权利请求的和解

（1）除下列情形以外，对证明是无效的权利请求或者抗辩不予主张或者放弃的，不是对价：

（a）由于事实或者法律具有不确定性，权利请求或者抗辩事实上是存在疑问的，或者

（b）不予主张或者放弃的一方有理由相信，权利请求或者抗辩可能被公平地认定为有效的。

（2）没有签署放弃权利请求或者抗辩的书面文书的义务，且文书签署是交易的对象的，即使签署人并没有主张权利请求或者抗辩，并且认为不存在有效的权利请求或者抗辩，文书的签署也构成对价。

§ 75. Exchange of Promise for Promise

Except as stated in §§ 76 and 77, a promise which is bargained for is consideration if, but only if, the promised performance would be consideration.

第 75 条　　以允诺交换允诺

除第 76 条和第 77 条所述规则以外，作为交易对象的允诺，只有（且只有）被允诺的履行是对价时才构成对价。

§ 76. Conditional Promise

（1）A conditional promise is not consideration if the promisor knows at the time of making the promise that the condition cannot occur.

（2）A promise conditional on a performance by the promisor is a promise of alternative performances within § 77 unless occurrence of the condition is also promised.

第 76 条　　附条件的允诺

（1）允诺人作出允诺时知道条件不可能成就的，附条件的允诺不是对价。

（2）以允诺人的某履行为条件的允诺是第 77 条所述的允诺替代履行，但

同时允诺了条件的成就的除外。

§ 77. Illusory and Alternative Promises

A promise or apparent promise is not consideration if by its terms the promisor or purported promisor reserves a choice of alternative performances unless

(a) each of the alternative performances would have been consideration if it a-lone had been bargained for; or

(b) one of the alternative performances would have been consideration and there is or appears to the parties to be a substantial possibility that before the promisor exercises his choice events may eliminate the alternatives which would not have been consideration.

第 77 条　虚幻的与替代的允诺

除下列情形以外，允诺人或者宣称允诺人在允诺或者表面允诺的条款中保留选择替代履行的权利的，允诺或者表面允诺不是对价：

（a）每个替代履行如果单独作为交易对象都构成对价的，或者

（b）有一个替代履行构成对价，且在允诺人行使选择权之前有实质性的可能，或者在当事人看来会有实质性的可能，不构成对价的替代履行会因事件的发生归于消灭的。

§ 78. Voidable and Unenforceable Promises

The fact that a rule of law renders a promise voidable or unenforceable does not prevent it from being consideration.

第 78 条　可撤销的与不可强制执行的允诺

法律规则使得允诺可撤销或者不可强制执行的，不阻却允诺构成对价。

§ 79. Adequacy of Consideration; Mutuality of Obligation

If the requirement of consideration is met, there is no additional requirement of

(a) a gain, advantage, or benefit to the promisor or a loss, disadvantage, or detriment to the promisee; or

(b) equivalence in the values exchanged; or

(c) "mutuality of obligation."

第 79 条　对价的充分性；义务的相互性

对价要求已经满足的，不再要求下列事项：

(a) 允诺人有得、有利或者可以受益，或者受诺人有失、不利或者产生损害；或者

(b) 交换的等值；或者

(c) "义务的相互性"。

§ 80. Multiple Exchanges

(1) There is consideration for a set of promises if what is bargained for and given in exchange would have been consideration for each promise in the set if exchanged for that promise alone.

(2) The fact that part of what is bargained for would not have been consideration if that part alone had been bargained for does not prevent the whole from being consideration.

第 80 条　多重交换

(1) 允诺组中的每一个允诺单独用于交换时，受诺人给予的作为交易对象的交换都构成对价的，允诺组存在对价。

(2) 部分交易对象单独用于交易时不构成对价的，不阻却交易对象整体构成对价。

§ 81. Consideration as Motive or Inducting Cause

（1）The fact that what is bargained for does not of itself induce the making of a promise does not prevent it from being consideration for the promise.

（2）The fact that a promise does not of itself induce a performance or return promise does not prevent the performance or return promise from being consideration for the promise.

第 81 条　作为动机或者诱因的对价

（1）交易对象并不自然诱使允诺作出的，不阻却交易对象构成允诺的对价。

（2）允诺并不自然诱使履行或者回报允诺作出的，不阻却履行或者回报允诺构成允诺的对价。

TOPIC 2.　CONTRACTS WITHOUT CONSIDERATION
第二节　无需对价的合同

§ 82. Promise to Pay Indebtedness; Effect on the Statute of Limitations

（1）A promise to pay all or part of an antecedent contractual or quasi-contractual indebtedness owed by the promisor is binding if the indebtedness is still enforceable or would be except for the effect of a statute of limitations.

（2）The following facts operate as such a promise unless other facts indicate a different intention:

（a）A voluntary acknowledgment to the obligee, admitting the present existence of the antecedent indebtedness; or

（b）A voluntary transfer of money, a negotiable instrument, or other thing by the obligor to the obligee, made as interest on or part payment of or collateral security for the antecedent indebtedness; or

（c）A statement to the obligee that the statute of limitations will not be pleaded as a defense.

第 82 条 允诺偿还债务；时效法的效力

（1）允诺部分或者全部偿还允诺人所欠的先前合同或者准合同债务的，如果债务仍然可以强制执行，或者若无时效法的规定仍然可以强制执行时，允诺具有约束力。

（2）除其他事实表明不同意思之外，下列事实构成上述允诺：

（a）向权利人主动承认先前债务仍然存在的；或者

（b）义务人主动向权利人移转金钱、流通票据或者其他物品，作为先前债务的利息、部分支付或者附加担保的；或者

（c）向权利人作出不援引时效法作为抗辩的陈述的。

§ 83. Promise to Pay Indebtedness Discharged in Bankruptcy

An express promise to pay all or part of an indebtedness of the promisor, discharged or dischargeable in bankruptcy proceedings begun before the promise is made, is binding.

第 83 条 允诺偿还破产程序中解除的债务

明确作出偿还允诺前开始的破产程序中被解除或者可以解除的全部或者部分允诺人债务的，允诺具有约束力。

§ 84. Promise to Perform a Duty in Spite of Non-Occurrence of a Condition

（1）Except as stated in Subsection（2）, a promise to perform all or part of a conditional duty under an antecedent contract in spite of the non-occurrence of the condition is binding, whether the promise is made before or after the time for the condition to occur, unless

（a）occurrence of the condition was a material part of the agreed exchange for the performance of the duty and the promisee was under no duty that it occur; or

（b）uncertainty of the occurrence of the condition was an element of the risk assumed by the promisor.

(2) If such a promise is made before the time for the occurrence of the condition has expired and the condition is within the control of the promisee or a beneficiary, the promisor can make his duty again subject to the condition by notifying the promisee or beneficiary of his intention to do so if

(a) the notification is received while there is still a reasonable time to cause the condition to occur under the antecedent terms or an extension given by the promisor; and

(b) reinstatement of the requirement of the condition is not unjust because of a material change of position by the promisee or beneficiary; and

(c) the promise is not binding apart from the rule stated in Subsection (1).

第 84 条　即使条件不成就也履行义务的允诺

(1) 除第 (2) 款所述规则以外，允诺即使条件不成就也全部或者部分履行先前合同项下的附条件义务的，无论在规定的条件成就期限之前还是之后作出，允诺都有约束力，但下列情形除外：

(a) 条件的成就是用以换取该义务履行的约定交换中的重要部分，且受诺人对条件的成就不承担义务的；或者

(b) 条件成就的不确定性是允诺人所承担风险中的因素的。

(2) 允诺是在条件成就期限届满之前作出，并且条件处于受诺人或者受益人控制之下的，如果有下列情形，允诺人可以向受诺人或者受益人通知其意图后重新使得其义务取决于条件的成就：

(a) 根据先前合同的条款或者允诺人给予的展期，在仍然有合理时间使得条件成就的情况下收到允诺人通知的；且

(b) 恢复对条件的要求不会因为受诺人或者受益人地位的重大改变而造成不公平的；且

(c) 除第 (1) 款所述规则以外，允诺不具有约束力的。

§ 85. Promise to Perform a Voidable Duty

Except as stated in § 93, a promise to perform all or part of an antecedent contract of the promisor, previously voidable by him, but not avoided prior to the making of the promise, is binding.

第 85 条 允诺履行可撤销义务

除第 93 条所述规则以外，允诺人之前可以撤销的先前合同没有撤销，随后又允诺全部或者部分履行的，允诺有约束力。

§ 86. Promise For Benefit Received

(1) A promise made in recognition of a benefit previously received by the promisor from the promisee is binding to the extent necessary to prevent injustice.

(2) A promise is not binding under Subsection (1)

(a) if the promisee conferred the benefit as a gift or for other reasons the promisor has not been unjustly enriched; or

(b) to the extent that its value is disproportionate to the benefit.

第 86 条 因为收到的利益而允诺

(1) 允诺人鉴于之前从受诺人处获取的利益而作出允诺的，在避免不公正所必须的范围内有约束力。

(2) 有下列情形的，第 (1) 款规定的允诺没有约束力：

(a) 受诺人赠予该利益的，或者由于其他原因允诺人并没有不当得利的；或者

(b) 允诺价值与利益不成比例的。

§ 87. Option Contract

(1) An offer is binding as an option contract if it

(a) is in writing and signed by the offeror, recites a purported consideration for the making of the offer, and proposes an exchange on fair terms within a reasonable time; or

(b) is made irrevocable by statute.

（2）An offer which the offeror should reasonably expect to induce action or for-bearance of a substantial character on the part of the offeree before acceptance and which does induce such action or forbearance is binding as an option contract to the extent necessary to avoid injustice.

第87条　选择权合同

（1）有下列情形的，要约是有约束力的选择权合同：

（a）采用书面形式并经要约人签字，记载了为要约提供的宣称对价，并提出在合理期限内进行条款公平的交换的；或者

（b）制定法规定不可撤销的。

（2）要约人能够合理预见，其要约会诱使受要约人在承诺之前采取实质性的行为或者不行为，且确实诱使这种行为或者不行为发生的，在避免不公正所必需的范围内，要约是有约束力的选择权合同。

§ 88. Guaranty

A promise to be surety for the performance of a contractual obligation, made to the obligee, is binding if

（a）the promise is in writing and signed by the promisor and recites a purported consideration; or

（b）the promise is made binding by statute; or

（c）the promisor should reasonably expect the promise to induce action or for-bearance of a substantial character on the part of the promisee or a third person, and the promise does induce such action or forbearance.

第88条　保证

向权利人作出的保证[1]合同义务履行的允诺，在下列情形下具有约

---

[1] 保证（surety），此处为担保法意义上的"保证"，与guaranty（如本条英文标题）是近义词，后者也译为"保证"，两词在本条中似乎并无不同。根据有关资料，surety含义有广狭之分，广义的surety既包括第一位（primary）责任，也包括第二位（secondary）责任，狭义的则只有第一位责任；而guaranty主要指第二位责任，最常用的语境是金融领域，很少用于法律语境之外。另，gurantee也是常见的近义词。参见Garner（2009）有关词条。也请比较第251条注释。

束力：

（a）允诺采用书面形式并经允诺人签字，且记载了宣称对价的；或者

（b）制定法使得允诺有约束力的；或者

（c）允诺人能够合理预见，其允诺会诱使受诺人或者第三人采取实质性的行为或者不行为，且确实诱使此种行为或者不行为发生的。

§ 89. Modification of Executory Contract

A promise modifying a duty under a contract not fully performed on either side is binding

（a）if the modification is fair and equitable in view of circumstances not anticipated by the parties when the contract was made; or

（b）to the extent provided by statute; or

（c）to the extent that justice requires enforcement in view of material change of position in reliance on the promise.

第89条 待履行合同的变更

变更任何一方都没有完全履行的合同项下义务的允诺，在下列情形下具有约束力：

（a）鉴于合同订立时当事人都没有预料到的新情况，变更是公平公正的；或者

（b）在制定法规定的范围内；或者

（c）鉴于信赖允诺引起的地位的重大改变，强制执行允诺是在公正所需的范围之内。

§ 90. Promise Reasonably Inducing Action or Forbearance

（1）A promise which the promisor should reasonably expect to induce action or forbearance on the part of the promisee or a third person and which does induce such action or forbearance is binding if injustice can be avoided only by enforcement of the promise. The remedy granted for breach may be limited as justice requires.

（2）A charitable subscription or a marriage settlement is binding under Subsection（1）without proof that the promise induced action or forbearance.

第 90 条　合理诱使行为或者不行为的允诺

（1）允诺人能够合理预见，其允诺会诱使受诺人或者第三人采取行为或者不行为，并且确实诱使此种行为或者不行为产生的，如果只有强制执行允诺才能避免不公正，则允诺具有约束力。因违背允诺而判予的救济可以按照公正的要求予以限制。

（2）慈善捐赠或者婚姻财产协议根据第（1）款的规则是有约束力的，不需要证明允诺诱使了行为或者不行为的产生。

§ 91. Effect of Promises Enumerated in §§ 82−90 When Conditional

If a promise within the terms of §§ 82−90 is in terms conditional or performable at a future time the promisor is bound thereby, but performance becomes due only upon the occurrence of the condition or upon the arrival of the specified time.

第 91 条　第 82~90 条所列允诺附条件时的效力

属于第 82~90 条范围内的允诺的条款是附条件的，或者是在将来的时间履行的，允诺人受到允诺的约束，但只有条件成就时或者指定时间到来时才应予履行。

§ 92. To Whom Promises Enumerated in §§ 82−85 Must Be Made

The new promise referred to in §§ 82−85 is not binding unless it is made to a person who is then an obligee of the antecedent duty.

第 92 条　第 82~85 条所列允诺必须向谁作出

第 82~85 条所指的新允诺，只有向作出允诺时还是先前义务的权利人的人作出时才有约束力。

§ 93. Promises Enumerated in §§ 82-85 Made in Ignorance of Facts

A promise within the terms of §§ 82 – 85 is not binding unless the promisor knew or had reason to know the essential facts of the previous transaction to which the promise relates, but his knowledge of the legal effect of the facts is immaterial.

第93条 第82~85 条所列允诺在不知晓事实的情况下作出时

属于第82~85 条范围内的允诺，只有允诺人知道或者有理由知道与允诺有关的先前交易的基本事实时才有约束力，但对事实产生的法律效力的知晓并不重要。

§ 94. Stipulations

A promise or agreement with reference to a pending judicial proceeding, made by a party to the proceeding or his attorney, is binding without consideration. By statute or rule of court such an agreement is generally binding only

(a) if it is in writing and signed by the party or attorney, or

(b) if it is made or admitted in the presence of the court, or

(c) to the extent that justice requires enforcement in view of material change of position in reliance on the promise or agreement.

第94条 诉讼协议

司法程序当事人或者当事人的律师针对未决司法程序作出的允诺或者协议，没有对价也有约束力。依据制定法或者法院判决，此种协议一般只在下列情形具有约束力：

（a）采用书面形式并由当事人或者当事人的律师签字的，或者

（b）当庭作出或者当庭承认的，或者

（c）鉴于信赖允诺或者协议而产生的重大地位改变，在公正要求强制执行的范围之内的。

TOPIC 3. CONTRACTS UNDER SEAL; WRITING AS A STATUTORY SUBSTITUTE FOR THE SEAL

第三节 盖印合同；书面形式作为盖印的法定替代

§ 95. Requirements for Sealed Contract or Written Contract or Instrument

（1）In the absence of statute a promise is binding without consideration if

（a）it is in writing and sealed; and

（b）the document containing the promise is delivered; and

（c）the promisor and promisee are named in the document or so described as to be capable of identification when it is delivered.

（2）When a statute provides in effect that a written contract or instrument is binding without consideration or that lack of consideration is an affirmative defense to an action on a written contract or instrument, in order to be subject to the statute a promise must either

（a）be expressed in a document signed or otherwise assented to by the promisor and delivered; or

（b）be expressed in a writing or writings to which both promisor and promisee manifest assent.

第 95 条 盖印合同或者书面合同或者文书的要求

（1）若无制定法规定，允诺只在下列情形下即使没有对价也会产生约束力：

（a）采用书面形式并经盖印的；且

（b）包含允诺的文件被交付的；且

（c）文件交付时，文件记载了允诺人和受诺人，或者其描述足以识别允诺人和受诺人的。

（2）制定法规定，书面合同或者书面文书即使没有对价也有约束力的，或者在涉及书面合同或者书面文书的诉讼中，缺乏对价是肯定性答辩的，如果适用该制定法，允诺必须满足下列条件：

（a）表述文件经允诺人签字或者以其他方式表示同意，并交付；或者

（b）由一份或者多份书面形式表述并经允诺人和受诺人作出同意表示。

§ 96. What Constitutes a Seal

（1）A seal is a manifestation in tangible and conventional form of an intention that a document be sealed.

（2）A seal may take the form of a piece of wax, a wafer or other substance affixed to the document or of an impression made on the document.

（3）By statute or decision in most States in which the seal retains significance a seal may take the form of a written or printed seal, word, scrawl or other sign.

第 96 条　何为印记

（1）印记，是指以有形的惯常形式体现的将文件盖印的意思表示。

（2）印记的形式可以是附着于文件之上的封蜡、干胶或者其他物质，也可以是在文件上加盖的压印。

（3）在盖印仍然具有意义的大多数州，制定法或者判决规定，盖印可以采用书面或者印刷的印记、文字、草签或者其他符号的形式。

§ 97. When a Promise is Sealed

A written promise is sealed if the promisor affixes or impresses a seal on the document or adopts a seal already thereon.

第 97 条　允诺何时为盖印允诺

书面允诺的允诺人使印记附着或者加盖于文件之上，或者采用了文件原有印记的，是盖印允诺。

§ 98. Adoption of a Seal by Delivery

Unless extrinsic circumstances manifest a contrary intention, the delivery of a written promise by the promisor amounts to the adoption of any seal then on the document which has apparent reference to his signature or to the signature of another party to the document.

第 98 条　因交付而采用印记

除非外部情形具有相反的意思，允诺人交付书面允诺的，等同于采用了文件上当时已有的、表面指称其签字或者文件他方当事人签字的印记。

§ 99. Adoption of the Same Seal by Several Parties

Any number of parties to the same instrument may adopt one seal.

第 99 条　多方当事人采用同一印记

同一文书任何数目的当事人均可采用一个印记。

§ 100. Recital of Sealing or Delivery

A recital of the sealing or of the delivery of a written promise is not essential to its validity as a contract under seal and is not conclusive of the fact of sealing or delivery unless a statute makes a recital of sealing the equivalent of a seal.

第 100 条　对盖印或者交付的陈述

对书面允诺盖印或者交付的陈述，并不是盖印合同的效力所必需，也不是盖印或者交付的确证，但制定法规定盖印陈述等同于印记的除外。

§ 101. Delivery

A written promise, sealed or unsealed, may be delivered by the promisor in escrow, conditionally to the promisee, or unconditionally.

第 101 条　交付

无论是否盖印，书面允诺都可以由允诺人以第三方存管的方式附条件交付于受诺人，也可以不附条件。

§ 102. Unconditional Delivery

A written promise is delivered unconditionally when the promisor puts it out of his possession and manifests an intention that it is to take effect at once according to its terms.

第 102 条　无条件交付

允诺人将书面允诺置于脱离自己控制之处，并作出允诺按其条款立即生效的意思表示时，是无条件交付。

§ 103. Delivery in Escrow; Conditional Delivery to the Promisee

（1）A written promise is delivered in escrow by the promisor when he puts it into the possession of a person other than the promisee without reserving a power of revocation and manifests an intention that the document is to take effect according to its terms upon the occurrence of a stated condition but not otherwise.

（2）A written promise is delivered conditionally to the promisee when the promisor puts it into the possession of the promisee without reserving a power of revocation and manifests an intention that the document is to take effect according to its terms upon the occurrence of a stated condition but not otherwise.

（3）Delivery of a written promise in escrow or its conditional delivery to the promisee has the same effect as unconditional delivery would have if the requirement of the condition were expressed in the writing.

（4）In the absence of a statute modifying the significance of a seal, delivery of a sealed promise in escrow or its conditional delivery to the promisee is irrevocable for the time specified by the promisor for the occurrence of the condition, or , if no time is specified, for a reasonable time.

第 103 条　第三方存管交付；附条件交付受诺人

（1）允诺人将书面允诺置于受诺人以外的他人控制之中，自己不保留撤销权，并表示所载条件一经成就允诺即可按其条款生效，且别无其他生效方式的，是以第三方存管的方式交付。

（2）允诺人将书面允诺文件置于受诺人控制之中，自己不保留撤销权，并表示所载条件一经成就允诺即可按其条款生效，且别无其他生效方式的，是向受诺人附条件交付。

（3）以第三方存管方式交付书面允诺，或者向受诺人附条件交付，其效力都等同于该书面形式中记载了条件要求时的无条件交付。

（4）若无制定法对印记意义予以修订，将盖印允诺以第三方存管方式交付于受诺人，或者附条件交付于受诺人的，在允诺人指定的条件成就期间内，或者没有指定期间时在合理的期限内，交付是不可撤销的。

§ 104. Acceptance or Disclaimer by the Promisee

（1）Neither acceptance by the promisee nor knowledge by him of the existence of a promise is essential to the formation of a contract by the delivery of a written promise which is binding without consideration.

（2）A promisee who has not manifested assent to a written promise may, within a reasonable time after learning of its existence and terms, render it inoperative by disclaimer.

（3）Acceptance or disclaimer is irrevocable.

第 104 条　受诺人的承诺或者弃权

（1）交付无对价也有约束力的书面允诺成立合同的，无论受诺人对允诺的承诺，还是受诺人对允诺存在的知晓，都不是合同成立所必需。

（2）受诺人尚未对书面允诺表示同意的，在得知允诺的存在和允诺条款后的合理时间内，可以通过弃权而使之不产生效力。

（3）承诺或者弃权是不可撤销的。

§ 105. Acceptance Where Return Promise is Contemplated

Where a conveyance or a document containing a promise also purports to contain a return promise by the grantee or promisee, acceptance by the grantee or promisee is essential to create any contractual obligation other than an option contract binding on the grantor or promisor.

第 105 条　期待回报允诺时的承诺

财产转让文书或者载有允诺的文件也宣称包含受让人或者受诺人的回报允诺的，受让人或者受诺人的承诺为创设合同义务所必需，但约束转让人或者允诺人的选择权合同除外。

§ 106. What Amounts to Acceptance of Instrument

Acceptance of a conveyance or of a document containing a promise is a manifestation of assent to the terms thereof made, either before or after delivery, in accordance with any requirements imposed by the grantor or promisor. If the acceptance occurs before delivery and is not binding as an option contract, it is revocable until the moment of delivery.

第 106 条　何为对文书的承诺

对财产转让文书或者载有允诺的文件的承诺，是指在文书或者文件交付之前或者之后，按照转让人或者允诺人的规定对其条款作出的同意表示。承诺发生在交付之前且不构成具有约束力的选择权合同的，在交付之前可以撤销。

§ 107. Creation of Unsealed Contract by Acceptance by Promisee

Where a grantee or promisee accepts a sealed document which purports to contain a return promise by him, he makes the return promise. But if he does not sign or seal the document his promise is not under seal, and whether it is binding depends on the rules governing unsealed contracts.

第 107 条　受诺人的承诺创设非盖印合同

受让人或者受诺人对宣称载有他的回报允诺的盖印文件进行承诺的，即为作出了回报允诺。但他没有在文件上签字或者盖章的，回报允诺不是盖印允诺，是否有约束力取决于调整非盖印合同的规则。

§ 108. Requirement of Naming or Describing Promisor and Promisee

A promise under seal is not binding without consideration unless both the promisor and the promisee are named in the document or so described as to be capable of identification when it is delivered.

第 108 条　指明或者描述允诺人和受诺人

只有文件在交付时记载了允诺人和受诺人双方，或者其描述足以识别允诺人和受诺人双方的，盖印允诺才在没有对价时产生约束力。

§ 109. Enforcement of a Sealed Contract by Promisee Who Does Not Sign or Seal it

The promisee of a promise under seal is not precluded from enforcing it as a sealed contract because he has not signed or sealed the document, unless his doing so was a condition of the delivery, whether or not the document contains a promise by him.

第 109 条　没有签字或者盖印的受诺人强制执行盖印合同

无论文件是否包含受诺人的允诺，盖印允诺的受诺人不因未在文件上签字或者盖印而被阻止将盖印允诺作为盖印合同强制执行，但签字或者盖印是文件交付条件的除外。

第五章

反欺诈法

Chapter 5

THE STATUTE OF FRAUDS

§ 110. Classes of Contracts Covered

(1) The following classes of contracts are subject to a statute, commonly called the Statute of Frauds, forbidding enforcement unless there is a written memorandum or an applicable exception:

(a) a contract of an executor or administrator to answer for a duty of his decedent (the executor-administrator provision);

(b) a contract to answer for the duty of another (the suretyship provision);

(c) a contract made upon consideration of marriage (the marriage provision);

(d) a contract for the sale of an interest in land (the land contract provision);

(e) a contract that is not to be performed within one year from the making thereof (the one-year provision).

(2) The following classes of contracts, which were traditionally subject to the Statute of Frauds, are now governed by Statute of Frauds provisions of the Uniform Commercial Code:

(a) a contract for the sale of goods for the price of $500 or more (Uniform Commercial Code § 2-201);

(b) a contract for the sale of securities (Uniform Commercial Code § 8-319);

(c) a contract for the sale of personal property not otherwise covered, to the extent of enforcement by way of action or defense beyond $5,000 in amount or value of remedy (Uniform Commercial Code § 1-206).

(3) In addition the Uniform Commercial Code requires a writing signed by the debtor for an agreement which creates or provides for a security interest in personal property or fixtures not in the possession of the secured party.

(4) Statutes in most states provide that no acknowledgement or promise is sufficient evidence of a new or continuing contract to take a case out of the operation of a statute of limitations unless made in some writing signed by the party to be charged, but that the statute does not alter the effect of any payment of principal or interest.

（5）In many states other classes of contracts are subject to a requirement of a writing.

第 110 条　调整的合同类别

（1）下述各类合同应遵守通常称为"反欺诈法"的制定法的规定，除有书面备忘录或者可适用的例外以外，禁止强制执行：

（a）遗产执行人或者遗产管理人为被继承人承担义务的合同（遗产执行人—管理人条款）；

（b）为他人承担义务的合同（保证条款）；

（c）以婚姻为对价的合同（婚姻条款）；

（d）出售土地权益的合同（土地合同条款）；

（e）自合同签订起一年之内不能履行完成的合同（一年条款）。

（2）下述各类合同传统上须遵守反欺诈法，现在由《统一商法典》的反欺诈条款进行调整：

（a）价款为 500 美元或者以上的货物销售合同（《统一商法典》第 2-201 条）；

（b）证券销售合同（《统一商法典》第 8-319 条）；

（c）其他没有规定的动产买卖合同，经诉讼或者抗辩而强制执行的救济数额或者价值超过 5000 美元的（《统一商法典》第 1-206 条）。

（3）另外，在有担保的债权人不占有的动产或者不动产附着物上创设或者规定担保权益的协议，《统一商法典》要求采用书面形式并由债务人签字。

（4）大多数州的制定法规定，只有以书面形式制作并经被要求承担义务的一方签字的确认或者允诺，才是使得案件时效中断的新合同或者持续性合同[1]的充分证据[2]，但时效法并不改变任何支付本金或者利息的效力。

（5）在许多州，也有其他类别的合同必须遵守书面形式要求。

---

　〔1〕　持续性合同（continuing contract）是"一种未给付的合同"，"因其须在一定期间分阶段履行，故得名"（薛波 2003：311）。

　〔2〕　充分证据（sufficient evidence）是指足以让追求真理、毫无偏见的人信服的证据 Garner（2009：639）。另见第 249 条注释 2。

TOPIC 1. THE EXECUTOR–ADMINISTRATOR PROVISION
第一节　遗产执行人—管理人条款

§ 111. Contract of Executor or Administrator

A contract of an executor or administrator to answer personally for a duty of his decedent is within the Statute of Frauds if a similar contract to answer for the duty of a living person would be within the Statute as a contract to answer for the duty of another.

第 111 条　遗产执行人或者管理人合同

为生者承担义务的类似合同是反欺诈法调整的为他人承担义务的合同，遗产执行人或者管理人个人为被继承人承担义务的合同属于反欺诈法的调整范围。

TOPIC 2. THE SURETYSHIP PROVISION
第二节　保证条款

§ 112. Requirement of Suretyship

A contract is not within the Statute of Frauds as a contract to answer for the duty of another unless the promisee is an obligee of the other's duty, the promisor is a surety for the other, and the promisee knows or has reason to know of the suretyship relation.

第 112 条　保证要求

只有受诺人是对方义务的权利人，允诺人是对方的保证人，且受诺人知道或者有理由知道保证关系存在的，合同才属于反欺诈法规定的为他人承担义务的合同。

§ 113. Promises of the Same Performance for the Same Consideration

Where promises of the same performance are made by two persons for a consideration which inures to the benefit of only one of them, the promise of the other is within the Statute of Frauds as a contract to answer for the duty of another, whether or not the promise is in terms conditional on default by the one to whose benefit the consideration inures, unless

(a) the other is not a surety for the one to whose benefit the consideration inures; or

(b) the promises are in terms joint and do not create several duties or joint and several duties; or

(c) the promisee neither knows nor has reason to know that the consideration does not inure to the benefit of both promisors.

第 113 条　为同一对价允诺同一履行

除下列情形以外，两人为了只让一人受益的对价而允诺同一履行的，另一人的允诺属于反欺诈法规定的为他人承担义务的合同，无论其条款是否规定以对价受益人的违约为条件：

(a) 另一人并非对价受益人的保证人的；或者

(b) 两人的允诺就条款而言是共同的，并未创设分别义务或者连带义务；或者

(c) 受诺人不知道，也没有理由知道对价并不是使两个允诺人都受益的。

§ 114. Independent Duty of Promisor

A contract to perform or otherwise to satisfy all or part of a duty of a third person to the promisee is not within the Statute of Frauds as a contract to answer for the duty of another if, by the terms of the promise when it is made, performance thereof can involve no more than

(a) the application of funds or property held by the promisor for the purpose, or （b）performance of any other duty owing, irrespective of his promise, by the promisor to the promisee, or

（c）performance of a duty which is either owing, irrespective of his promise, by the promisor to the third person, or which the promisee reasonably believes to be so owing.

第114条 允诺人的个人单独义务

允诺作出时的条款表明，允诺的履行仅会涉及下列情形的，履行或者以其他方式清偿第三人对受诺人所负的全部或者部分义务的合同，不属于反欺诈法规定的为他人承担义务的合同：

（a）使用允诺人为此目的持有的基金或者财产的，或者

（b）履行允诺人对受诺人应予履行的、与其允诺无关的任何其他义务的，或者

（c）履行允诺人对第三人应予履行的、与其允诺无关的义务，或者受诺人合理地认为存在这样的义务的。

§ 115. Novation

A contract that is itself accepted in satisfaction of a previously existing duty of a third person to the promisee is not within the Statute of Frauds as a contract to answer for the duty of another.

第115条 更新

合同本身的承诺是为了清偿第三人对受诺人的先前义务的，不属于反欺诈法规定的为他人承担义务的合同。

§ 116. Main Purpose; Advantage to Surety

A contract that all or part of a duty of a third person to the promisee shall be satisfied is not within the Statute of Frauds as a promise to answer for the duty of another if the consideration for the promise is in fact or apparently desired by the promisor mainly for his own economic advantage, rather than in order to benefit the third person. If, however, the consideration is merely a premium for insurance, the contract is within the Statute.

第116条　主要目的；保证人得利

允诺人寻求的对价，事实上或者表面上主要是服务于允诺人自身经济利益，而非让第三人受益的，清偿第三人对受诺人所负的全部或者部分义务的合同不属于反欺诈法规定的为他人承担义务的合同。但对价仅仅为保险费的，属于反欺诈法的调整范围。

§ 117. Promise to Sign a Written Contract of Suretyship

A promise to sign a written contract as a surety for the performance of a duty owed to the promisee or to sign a negotiable instrument for the accommodation of a person other than the promisee is within the Statute of Frauds.

第117条　签署书面保证合同的允诺

允诺签署书面合同以保证对受诺人义务的履行，或者签署可流通票据供受诺人以外的人融通之用的，属于反欺诈法的调整范围。

§ 118. Promise to Indemnify a Surety

A promise to indemnify against liability or loss made to induce the promisee to become a surety is not within the Statute of Frauds as a contract to answer for the duty of another.

第118条　补偿保证人的允诺

为诱使受诺人成为保证人而允诺补偿其所承担的责任或者损失的，不属于反欺诈法规定的为他人承担义务的合同。

§ 119. Assumption of Duty by Another

A contract not within the Statute of Frauds as a contract to answer for the duty of another when made is not brought within it by a subsequent promise of another person to assume performance of the duty as principal obligor.

第119条 他人承担义务

订立时不属于反欺诈法规定的为他人承担义务的合同，不因此后他人允诺以主义务人身份承担履行义务而受反欺诈法调整。

§ 120. Obligations on Negotiable Instruments

（1）An obligation on a negotiable instrument or a guaranty written on the instrument is not within the Statute of Frauds.

（2）A promise to pay a negotiable instrument, made by a party who has been or may be discharged by the holder's failure or delay in making presentment or giving notice of dishonor or in making protest, is not within the Statute of Frauds.

第120条 可流通票据的债务

（1）可流通票据的债务，或者书写于可流通票据之上的保证，不属于反欺诈法的调整范围。

（2）可流通票据的当事人由于持票人未能或者迟延提示票据、提供拒兑拒付通知或者提出异议，已经或者可能被免除义务的，该当事人支付可流通票据的允诺不属于反欺诈法的调整范围。

§ 121. Contract of Assignor or Factor

（1）A contract by the assignor of a right that the obligor of the assigned right will perform his duty is not within the Statute of Frauds as a contract to answer for the duty of another.

（2）A contract by an agent with his principal that a purchaser of the principal's goods through the agent will pay their price to the principal is not within the Statute of Frauds as a contract to answer for the duty of another.

第 121 条　转让人或者代销商合同

（1）权利[1]转让人的合同规定由被转让权利的义务人履行转让人义务的，不属于反欺诈法规定的为他人承担义务的合同。

（2）代理人与被代理人订立的合同规定，通过代理人购买被代理人货物的买方向被代理人支付价款的，不属于反欺诈法规定的为他人承担义务的合同。

§122. Contract to Buy a Right from the Obligee

A contract to purchase a right which the promisee has or may acquire against a third person is not within the Statute of Frauds as a contract to answer for the duty of another.

---

[1] 权利（right），本书将 right 译为"权利"，将"power"译为"权力"，但 right 与 power 在逻辑上并非界限分明的并列关系，而是互有交叉义项，具体释义请见 Garner（2009）。根据学者的观点，权利（right）一般包括五个要素：利益（interest）、主张（claim）、资格（entitlement）、力量［包括权威（power）和能力（capacity）］、自由（liberty）。参见夏勇："权利哲学的基本问题"，载《法学研究》2004 年第 3 期。根据霍菲尔德（Wesley Newcomb Hohfeld）的法律术语分析理论，如果在甲乙所处的法律关系中，甲要求乙做某事而遭到拒绝，甲可以提起能够逼迫乙去做此事的法律程序，那么甲就有权利（right）要求乙做某事，乙则有义务（duty）做此事，在此意义上 right 与 duty 是不可分的。与权利（right）不同，权力（power）是改变法律关系的能力（the capacity to change a legal relationship）。参见 Farnthworth：*Farnthworth on Contracts* 第三版卷一，2004 年版，第 205 页注释 3。如果甲有针对乙改变涉及某标的物的法律关系的权力（power），乙就有责任（liability）实现这一改变。有 power 和有 right 可能产生不同的结果。例如，附条件的动产分期买卖的买受人在最后一期付款到期时，如果他只是有取得所有权的 right，卖方有转移所有权的 duty，那么假如卖方拒绝转移所有权并返还买方已交货款，买方只能去起诉；而如果买方通过付清最后一期货款而有 power 取得所有权，则卖方就无法阻止此所有权的转移。另外，也存在对特定标的物有 legal power 而无 rights 或 privileges 的情况。参见 Brady：Law, Language and Logic：the Legal Philosophy of Wesley Newcomb Hohfeld［J］. Transactions of the Charles S. Peirce Society. 1972（4）。仅在英语中，right 与 power 就有这么复杂的区别和大量的不当使用（如 Hohfeld 所言），在英汉翻译中更是难以仅仅通过术语译名廓清两者的区别。在古汉语中，"权利"一词具有贬义，但自从丁韪良在《万国律例》中将"权利"确定为"rights"的译名之后，便成为具有中性和褒义的词语，并逐渐获得了广泛的应用（夏勇 2004）。根据上述文献，英文的两个单词和汉语的"权利"与"权力"不具有相应的等值关系，但翻译实务中，如果两个词同时出现于一个文本中，彼此的译名并不好区分，因此本书权且如此确定译名，请读者结合语境理解，若有好的处理方法敬请告知译者。

第 122 条　向权利人购买权利的合同

购买受诺人拥有的或者可能取得的针对第三人的权利的合同，不属于反欺诈法规定的为他人承担义务的合同。

§ 123. Contract to Discharge the Promisee's Duty

A contract to discharge a duty owed by the promisee to a third person is not within the Statute of Frauds as a contract to answer for the duty of another.

第 123 条　解除受诺人义务的合同

解除受诺人向第三人所负义务的合同，不属于反欺诈法规定的为他人承担义务的合同。

TOPIC 3.　THE MARRIAGE PROVISION
第三节　婚姻条款

§ 124. Contract Made Upon Consideration of Marriage

A promise for which all or part of the consideration is either marriage or a promise to marry is within the Statute of Frauds, except in the case of an agreement which consists only of mutual promises of two persons to marry each other.

第 124 条　以婚姻为对价订立的合同

以婚姻或者结婚允诺为全部或者部分对价的允诺属于反欺诈法的调整范围，但双方仅仅互为结婚允诺的协议除外。

TOPIC 4. THE LAND CONTRACT PROVISION
第四节　土地合同条款

§ 125. Contract to Transfer, Buy, or Pay for an Interest in Land

（1）A promise to transfer to any person any interest in land is within the Statute of Frauds.

（2）A promise to buy any interest in land is within the Statute of Frauds, irrespective of the person to whom the transfer is to be made.

（3）When a transfer of an interest in land has been made, a promise to pay the price, if originally within the Statute of Frauds, ceases to be within it unless the promised price is itself in whole or in part an interest in land.

（4）Statutes in most states except from the land contract and one-year provisions of the Statute of Frauds short-term leases and contracts to lease, usually for a term not longer than one year.

第 125 条　转让、购买土地权益的合同或者支付土地权益款项的合同

（1）向任何人转让任何土地权益的允诺属于反欺诈法的调整范围。

（2）购买任何土地权益的允诺属于反欺诈法的调整范围，无论权益受让人是何人。

（3）土地权益完成转让之后，本来属于反欺诈法调整范围的支付价款的允诺不再受其调整，但允诺的价款本身全部或者部分是土地权益的除外。

（4）大多数州的制定法将短期租赁[1]和租赁合同（期限通常不超过一年）排除于反欺诈法的土地合同条款和一年条款之外。

---

〔1〕　短期租赁（short-term leases），lease 译为"租赁"，也常译为"租约"，既有产权的契据转让性质，又有合同性质。参见"重述"原文本条的评论 b，以及斯普兰克林：《美国财产法精解》，钟书峰译，北京大学出版社 2009 年版，第 210 页、第 220 页。

§ 126. Contract to Procure Transfer or to Act as Agent

（1）A contract to procure the transfer of an interest in land by a person other than the promisor is within the Statute of Frauds.

（2）A contract to act as agent for another in endeavoring to procure the transfer of any interest in land by someone other than the promisor is not within the Statute of Frauds as a contract for the sale of an interest in land.

第 126 条　促成转让的合同或者代理合同

（1）促成允诺人之外的人转让土地权益的合同受反欺诈法的调整。

（2）作为他人的代理人努力促成允诺人之外的人转让土地权益的合同，不是反欺诈法调整的土地权益销售合同。

§ 127. Interest in Land

An interest in land within the meaning of the Statute is any right, privilege, power or immunity, or combination thereof, which is an interest in land under the law of property and is not "goods" within the Uniform Commercial Code.

第 127 条　土地权益

反欺诈法所称的土地权益，是指属于财产法规定的土地权益而非《统一商法典》所称"货物"的任何权利、特权、权力或者豁免，或者前述各项的组合。

§ 128. Boundary and Partition Agreements

（1）A contract between owners of adjoining tracts of land fixing a dividing boundary is within the Statute of Frauds but if the location of the boundary was honestly disputed the contract becomes enforceable notwithstanding the Statute when the agreed boundary has been marked or has been recognized in the subsequent use of the tracts.

（2）A contract by joint tenants or tenants in common to partition land into separate tracts for each tenant is within the Statute of Frauds but becomes enforceable notwithstanding the Statute as to each tract when possession of it is taken in severalty in accordance with the agreement.

第128条　土地划界和分割协议

（1）相邻地块的所有人划分地界的合同属于反欺诈法的调整范围，但地界的位置曾存在善意的争议的，新商定的地界已经做出标记或者在此后地块的使用中争议得以确认时，尽管有反欺诈法的规定，合同也可以强制执行。

（2）共同承租人或者混合共同承租人将土地划分为每个承租人分别所有的地块的合同，属于反欺诈法的调整范围，但每个地块已经按照协议分别占有时，尽管有反欺诈法的规定，对于每个地块合同都可以强制执行。

§ 129. Action in Reliance; Specific Performance

A contract for the transfer of an interest in land may be specifically enforced notwithstanding failure to comply with the Statute of Frauds if it is established that the party seeking enforcement, in reasonable reliance on the contract and on the continuing assent of the party against whom enforcement is sought, has so changed his position that injustice can be avoided only by specific enforcement.

第129条　因信赖而行为；具体履行

如果能够认定，请求强制执行的当事人对合同和被请求方的持续同意产生合理信赖且改变了自己的地位，只有具体强制执行才能避免不公正发生的，转让土地权益的合同即使不符合反欺诈法的规定也可以具体强制执行。

TOPIC 5. THE ONE-YEAR PROVISION
第五节　一年条款

§ 130. Contract Not to Be Performed Within a Year

(1) Where any promise in a contract cannot be fully performed within a year from the time the contract is made, all promises in the contract are within the Statute of Frauds until one party to the contract completes his performance.

(2) When one party to a contract has completed his performance, the one-year provision of the Statute does not prevent enforcement of the promises of other parties.

第 130 条　一年内不能履行完毕的合同

(1) 合同中的任何允诺自合同成立之日起一年内不能完全履行完毕的，合同所有的允诺都属于反欺诈法的调整范围，直至一方当事人完成己方履行为止。

(2) 合同一方当事人已经完成己方履行的，反欺诈法的一年条款不阻却对其他当事人允诺的强制执行。

TOPIC 6. SATISFACTION OF THE STATUTE BY A MEMORANDUM
第六节　使用备忘录满足反欺诈法的要求

§ 131. General Requisites of a Memorandum

Unless additional requirements are prescribed by the particular statute, a contract within the Statute of Frauds is enforceable if it is evidenced by any writing, signed by or on behalf of the party to be charged, which

(a) reasonably identifies the subject matter of the contract,

(b) is sufficient to indicate that a contract with respect thereto has been made between the parties or offered by the signer to the other party, and （c）states with reasonable certainty the essential terms of the unperformed promises in the contract.

第 131 条　备忘录的一般要求

除具体立法有额外要求的以外，有任何书面文件证明，书面文件经被要求强制执行的当事人或者其代表人签字且同时有下列情形的，受反欺诈法调整的合同可以强制执行：

（a）合理地确定了合同标的，

（b）充分表明当事人之间已经缔结了相关合同，或者签字人已经向对方当事人发出缔结合同的要约，且

（c）以合理的确定性陈述了合同中尚未履行的允诺的基本条款。

§ 132. Several Writings

The memorandum may consist of several writings if one of the writings is signed and the writings in the circumstances clearly indicate that they relate to the same transaction.

第 132 条　数个书面文件

数个书面文件之一已经签字，且情形清晰地表明所有文件是关于同一交易的，备忘录可以由数个书面文件构成。

§ 133. Memorandum Not Made as Such

Except in the case of a writing evidencing a contract upon consideration of marriage, the Statute may be satisfied by a signed writing not made as a memorandum of a contract.

第 133 条　不是作为备忘录制作的备忘录

除了以婚姻为对价的合同的书面证明以外，不是作为合同备忘录制作的经签字的书面文件也可以满足反欺诈法的要求。

§ 134. Signature

The signature to a memorandum may be any symbol made or adopted with an intention, actual or apparent, to authenticate the writing as that of the signer.

第 134 条 签字

备忘录的签字，可以是以证明书面文件是签字人所签为意思表示而制作或者采用的任何符号；意思表示可以是真实的，也可以是表面的。

§ 135. Who Must Sign

Where a memorandum of a contract within the Statute is signed by fewer than all parties to the contract and the Statute is not otherwise satisfied, the contract is enforceable against the signers but not against the others.

第 135 条 谁必须签字

属于反欺诈法调整的合同的备忘录，签字人数少于合同当事人总数，且没有通过其他形式满足反欺诈法要求的，合同可以对签字人强制执行，但不可以对其他人强制执行。

§ 136. Time of Memorandum

A memorandum sufficient to satisfy the Statute may be made or signed at any time before or after the formation of the contract.

第 136 条 备忘录的时间

充分符合反欺诈法要求的备忘录，可以在合同成立前后的任何时间制作或者签字。

§ 137. Loss or Destruction of a Memorandum

The loss or destruction of a memorandum does not deprive it of effect under the Statute.

第 137 条　备忘录丢失或者毁损

备忘录丢失或者毁损的，不丧失反欺诈法规定的效力。

TOPIC 7. CONSEQUENCES OF NON-COMPLIANCE
第七节　不符合反欺诈法的后果

§ 138. Unenforceability

Where a contract within the Statute of Frauds is not enforceable against the party to be charged by an action against him, it is not enforceable by a set-off or counter-claim in an action brought by him, or as a defense to a claim by him.

第 138 条　不可强制执行

属于反欺诈法调整的合同不可以对诉讼被告强制执行的，在被告提起的诉讼中，不会因为抵销[1]或者反诉而可以强制执行，也不会因为是对被告请求的抗辩而可以强制执行。

§ 139. Enforcement by Virtue of Action in Reliance

（1）A promise which the promisor should reasonably expect to induce action or forbearance on the part of the promisee or a third person and which does induce the action or forbearance is enforceable notwithstanding the Statute of Frauds if injustice can be avoided only by enforcement of the promise. The remedy granted for breach is to be limited as justice requires.

（2）In determining whether injustice can be avoided only by enforcement of the promise, the following circumstances are significant:

（a）the availability and adequacy of other remedies, particularly cancellation

---

〔1〕 抵销（set-off），译者认为，此处的"set-off"意同"set off"。薛波（2003）将 set off 解释为"在同一诉讼中被告以反请求在原告的请求限度内抵销原告的请求。抵销只适用于金钱债权，作为一种抗辩的依据，目的在于防止反诉，因此它不是独立的实体请求权，由法庭综合考虑一并审理"。

and restitution;

(b) the definite and substantial character of the action or forbearance in relation to the remedy sought;

(c) the extent to which the action or forbearance corroborates evidence of the making and terms of the promise, or the making and terms are otherwise established by clear and convincing evidence;

(d) the reasonableness of the action or forbearance;

(e) the extent to which the action or forbearance was foreseeable by the promisor.

第 139 条　因基于信赖的行为而强制执行

(1) 允诺人能够合理预见，其允诺会诱使受诺人或者第三人采取行为或者不行为，且确实诱使了行为或者不行为发生的，如果只有强制执行允诺才能避免不公正，则尽管有反欺诈法的规定，允诺也可以强制执行。因违反允诺而判予的救济限制在公正所要求的范围之内。

(2) 确定是否只有强制执行允诺才能避免不公正时，下列情形具有重要意义：

(a) 其他救济方式，尤其是撤销和返还，是否存在及其充分性；

(b) 与所请求的救济相比，行为或者不行为的确定性实质特征；

(c) 在多大程度上，行为或者不行为能够确证允诺作出和允诺条款的证据，或者允诺作出和允诺条款可以在其他方面被明白清楚且令人信服的证据所证明；

(d) 行为或者不行为的合理性；

(e) 在多大程度上允诺人能够预见行为或者不行为。

§ 140. Defense of Failure to Perform

The Statute of Frauds does not invalidate defenses based on the plaintiff's failure to perform a condition of his claim or defenses based on his present or prospective breach of the contract he seeks to enforce.

第 140 条　未履行抗辩

基于原告未履行其诉讼请求的条件的抗辩，或者基于原告对其请求强制执行的合同存在当前违约或者预期违约情况的抗辩，不因反欺诈法而无效。

§ 141. Action for Value of Performance Under Unenforceable Contract

（1）In an action for the value of performance under a contract, except as stated in Subsection（2）, the Statute of Frauds does not invalidate any defense which would be available if the contract were enforceable against both parties.

（2）Where a party to a contract which is unenforceable against him refuses either to perform the contract or to sign a sufficient memorandum, the other party is justified in suspending any performance for which he has not already received the agreed return, and such a suspension is not a defense in an action for the value of performance rendered before the suspension.

第 141 条　请求不可强制执行合同项下的已履行价值之诉

（1）除第（2）款所述规则以外，在请求合同项下的已履行价值之诉中，合同对双方当事人均可强制执行时存在的抗辩不因反欺诈法而无效。

（2）合同不可以针对某当事人强制执行时，该当事人拒绝履行合同，或者拒绝签订充分备忘录的，对方当事人可以中止尚未取得约定回报的任何履行，且在请求中止前给付的履行价值之诉中，中止不构成抗辩事由。

§ 142. Tort Liability for Acts Under Unenforceable Contract

Where because of the existence of a contract conduct would not be tortious, unenforceability of the contract under the Statute of Frauds does not make the conduct tortious if it occurs without notice of repudiation of the contract.

第 142 条　不可强制执行合同项下行为的侵权责任

合同存在则行为就不会构成侵权的，如果行为发生时并不知悉合同的拒绝履行，则反欺诈法规定的合同不可强制执行并不导致行为侵权。

§ 143. Unenforceable Contract as Evidence

The Statue of Frauds does not make an unenforceable contract inadmissible in evidence for any purpose other than its enforcement in violation of the Statute.

第 143 条 不可强制执行合同用作证据

除因违反反欺诈法而产生的强制执行问题以外，反欺诈法不影响不可强制执行合同为了任何目的用作证据的可采性。

§ 144. Effect of Unenforceable Contract as to Third Parties

Only a party to a contract or a transferee or successor of a party to the contract can assert that the contract is unenforceable under the Statute of Frauds.

第 144 条 不可强制执行合同对于第三人的效力

只有合同当事人，或者当事人的受让人或者继承人，才能按照反欺诈法主张合同不可强制执行。

§ 145. Effect of Full Performance

Where the promises in a contract have been fully performed by all parties, the Statute of Frauds does not affect the legal relations of the parties.

第 145 条 完全履行的效力

合同中的允诺均已由所有当事人完全履行完毕的，反欺诈法不影响当事人之间的法律关系。

§ 146. Rights of Competing Transferees of Property

（1）Where a contract to transfer property or a transfer was unenforceable against the transferor under the Statute of Frauds but subsequently becomes enforceable, the contract or transfer has whatever priority it would have had aside from the Statute of Frauds over an intervening contract by the transferor to transfer the same property to a third person.

(2) If the third person obtains title to the property by an enforceable transaction before the prior contract becomes enforceable, the prior contract is unenforceable against him and does not affect his title.

第 146 条 相互冲突的财产受让人的权利

(1) 财产转让合同或者财产转让按照反欺诈法本来不能对转让人强制执行，但此后又可以强制执行的，相对于转让人将同一财产转让给第三人的后来合同，先前合同或者财产转让具有若不存在反欺诈法规定时的所有优先权利。

(2) 先前合同可以强制执行之前，第三人通过可强制执行的交易取得了财产产权的，先前合同不可以对第三人强制执行，也不影响他的产权。

§ 147. Contract Containing Multiple Promises

(1) Where performance of the promises in a contract which subject it to the Statute of Frauds is exclusively beneficial to one party, that party by agreeing to forego the performance may render the remainder of the contract enforceable, but this rule does not apply to a contract to transfer property on the promisor's death.

(2) Where the promises in a contract which subject it to the Statute have become enforceable or where the duty to perform them has been discharged by performance or otherwise, the Statute does not prevent enforcement of the remaining promises.

(3) Except as stated in this Section, where some of the unperformed promises in a contract are unenforceable against a party under the Statute of Frauds, all the promises in the contract are unenforceable against him.

第 147 条 包含多个允诺的合同

(1) 使合同受到反欺诈法调整的允诺的履行只专使一方当事人受益的，该当事人放弃该履行可以使得合同剩余部分可强制执行，但本规则不适用于允诺人死亡时转让财产的合同。

（2）使合同受到反欺诈法调整的允诺已经可以强制执行的，或者由于履行或者其他原因这些允诺的履行义务已经解除的，反欺诈法不阻却剩余允诺的强制执行。

（3）除本条所述规则以外，由于反欺诈法的规定，合同中一些尚未履行的允诺针对某当事人不可强制执行的，合同所有的允诺对其均不可强制执行。

§ 148. Rescission by Oral Agreement

Notwithstanding the Statute of Frauds, all unperformed duties under an enforceable contract may be discharged by oral agreement of rescission. The Statute may, however, apply to a contract to rescind a transfer of property.

第 148 条　通过口头协议解约

尽管有反欺诈法的规定，可执行合同项下的所有未履行义务都可以通过口头解约协议解除。但是，反欺诈法可以适用于解除财产转让的合同。

§ 149. Oral Modification

（1）For the purpose of determining whether the Statute of Frauds applies to a contract modifying but not rescinding a prior contract, the second contract is treated as containing the originally agreed terms as modified. The Statute may, however, apply independently of the original terms to a contract to modify a transfer of property.

（2）Where the second contract is unenforceable by virtue of the Statute of Frauds and there has been no material change of position in reliance on it, the prior contract is not modified.

第 149 条　口头变更

（1）为了确定反欺诈法是否适用于变更但非解除先前合同的合同，第二个合同视为包含变更后的原始条款。但是反欺诈法可以独立于原始条款而适用于变更财产转让的合同。

（2）根据反欺诈法的规定第二个合同不可强制执行，且尚无因对该合同的信赖而产生地位的重大改变的，先前合同不产生变更的后果。

§ 150. Reliance on Oral Modification

Where the parties to an enforceable contract subsequently agree that all or part of a duty need not be performed or of a condition need not occur, the Statute of Frauds does not prevent enforcement of the subsequent agreement if reinstatement of the original terms would be unjust in view of a material change of position in reliance on the subsequent agreement.

第 150 条　信赖口头变更

可强制执行合同的当事人事后达成协议，同意某义务的全部或者部分不必履行，或者某条件的全部或者部分不必成就的，如果由于对事后协议的信赖产生地位的重大改变，因而恢复原始条款会有失公正，则反欺诈法不阻却事后协议的强制执行。

第六章

错　误

Chapter 6

MISTAKE

§ 151. Mistake Defined

A mistake is a belief that is not in accord with the facts.

第 151 条 错误的定义

错误，是指与事实不符的认识。

§ 152. When Mistake of Both Parties Makes a Contract Voidable

（1）Where a mistake of both parties at the time a contract was made as to a basic assumption on which the contract was made has a material effect on the agreed exchange of performances, the contract is voidable by the adversely affected party unless he bears the risk of the mistake under the rule stated in § 154.

（2）In determining whether the mistake has a material effect on the agreed exchange of performances, account is taken of any relief by way of reformation, restitution, or otherwise.

第 152 条 何时双方错误导致合同可撤销

（1）合同订立时，双方当事人都对合同据以订立的基本假设产生了对约定的履行交换有重大影响的错误的，受到不利影响的当事人可以撤销合同，但承担第 154 条所述规则规定的错误风险的情形除外。

（2）确定错误是否对约定的履行交换产生重大影响时，需要考虑通过合同重订[1]、返还或者其他方式提供的任何救济。

§ 153. When Mistake of One Party Makes a Contract Voidable

Where a mistake of one party at the time a contract was made as to a basic as-

---

[1] 重订（reformation），指由于错误或者误解导致文件出现表述错误或者内容缺失时，法庭应当事人的申请签发命令予以修改。参见张法连：《英美法律术语辞典》（英汉双解），上海外语教育出版社 2014 年版。本书根据英文原文的构词并结合全书术语间关系直译为"重订"，意为对有关条款的"重新订立"。

sumption on which he made the contract has a material effect on the agreed exchange of performances that is adverse to him, the contract is voidable by him if he does not bear the risk of the mistake under the rule stated in §154, and

(a) the effect of the mistake is such that enforcement of the contract would be unconscionable, or

(b) the other party had reason to know of the mistake or his fault caused the mistake.

第 153 条　何时单方错误导致合同可撤销

合同订立时，一方当事人对他据以订立合同的基本假设产生了对约定的履行交换有重大影响的错误且对其不利的，如果该当事人没有承担第 154 条所述规则规定的错误风险，并且有下列情形的，该当事人可以撤销合同：

(a) 错误的效力使得强制执行合同显失公平的，或者

(b) 对方当事人有理由知道该错误，或者错误是由对方当事人造成的。

§154. When a Party Bears the Risk of a Mistake

A party bears the risk of a mistake when

(a) the risk is allocated to him by agreement of the parties, or

(b) he is aware, at the time the contract is made, that he has only limited knowledge with respect to the facts to which the mistake relates but treats his limited knowledge as sufficient, or

(c) the risk is allocated to him by the court on the ground that it is reasonable in the circumstances to do so.

第 154 条　何时当事人承担了错误风险

在下列情形下，当事人承担了错误风险：

(a) 各方当事人约定将风险划分给他的，或者

(b) 合同订立之时就意识到对错误所涉事实所知有限，但仍然认为自己的有限知识已经足够的，或者

(c) 法院以当时情形下的合理选择为由将风险划分给他的。

§ 155. When Mistake of Both Parties as to Written Expression Justifies Reformation

Where a writing that evidences or embodies an agreement in whole or in part fails to express the agreement because of a mistake of both parties as to the contents or effect of the writing, the court may at the request of a party reform the writing to express the agreement, except to the extent that rights of third parties such as good faith purchasers for value will be unfairly affected.

第 155 条　何时关于书面表述的双方错误使得重订合理

证明或者体现全部或者部分协议的书面文件，由于双方当事人对其内容或者效力都存在错误认识，因而不能表达当事人协议的，法院可以应当事人要求进行重订，以便表述该协议，但诸如已付对价的善意购买人的第三人权利将会受到不公平影响的除外。

§ 156. Mistake as to Contract within the Statute of Frauds

If reformation of a writing is otherwise appropriate, it is not precluded by the fact that the contract is within the Statute of Frauds.

第 156 条　关于受反欺诈法调整的合同的错误

书面文件的重订在其他方面都是适当的，不因合同受反欺诈法调整而受阻却。

§ 157. Effect of Fault of Party Seeking Relief

A mistaken party's fault in failing to know or discover the facts before making the contract does not bar him from avoidance or reformation under the rules stated in this Chapter, unless his fault amounts to a failure to act in good faith and in accordance with reasonable standards of fair dealing.

第 157 条　寻求救济方存在过错的效力

发生错误的当事人在订立合同之前不知道或者未能发现事实真相的，这一过错并不妨碍他根据本章所述规则对合同进行撤销或者重订，但过错构成未能善意且依照公平交易的合理标准履行的除外。

§ 158. Relief Including Restitution

（1）In any case governed by the rules stated in this Chapter, either party may have a claim for relief including restitution under the rules stated in §§ 240 and 376.

（2）In any case governed by the rules stated in this Chapter, if those rules together with the rules stated in Chapter 16 will not avoid injustice, the court may grant relief on such terms as justice requires including protection of the parties' reliance interests.

第 158 条　包含返还在内的救济

（1）在适用本章所述规则的任何情况下，任意一方当事人都有权根据第 240 条和第 376 条所述规则请求包括返还在内的救济。

（2）在适用本章所述规则的情况下，本章规则以及第 16 章所述规则都无法避免不公的，法院可以根据公正的需要，判予包括保护当事人信赖权益在内的救济。

第七章

误述、胁迫与不当影响

Chapter 7

MISREPRESENTATION, DURESS AND UNDUE INFLUENCE

TOPIC 1. MISREPRESENTATION
第一节 误 述

§ 159. Misrepresentation Defined

A misrepresentation is an assertion that is not in accord with the facts.

第 159 条 误述的定义

误述，是指与事实不符的断言。

§ 160. When Action is Equivalent to an Assertion（Concealment）

Action intended or known to be likely to prevent another from learning a fact is equivalent to an assertion that the fact does not exist.

第 160 条 何时行为等于断言（隐瞒）

意图阻止，或者明知可能阻止他人获知事实的行为，等同于作出该事实不存在的断言。

§ 161. When Non-Disclosure Is Equivalent to an Assertion

A person's non-disclosure of a fact known to him is equivalent to an assertion that the fact does not exist in the following cases only：

（a）where he knows that disclosure of the fact is necessary to prevent some previous assertion from being a misrepresentation or from being fraudulent or material.

（b）where he knows that disclosure of the fact would correct a mistake of the other party as to a basic assumption on which that party is making the contract and if non-disclosure of the fact amounts to a failure to act in good faith and in accordance with reasonable standards of fair dealing.

（c）where he knows that disclosure of the fact would correct a mistake of the other party as to the contents or effect of a writing, evidencing or embodying an agreement in whole or in part.

（d）where the other person is entitled to know the fact because of a relation of trust and confidence between them.

第161条　何时不予披露等于断言

只有在下列情形下，不予披露自己已知事实等于作出该事实不存在的断言：

（a）知道披露该事实是阻止先前的断言成为误述或者变得具有欺诈性或重大性所必须的。

（b）知道披露该事实会纠正对方当事人正在订立的合同所基于的基本假设的错误，且不予披露将会构成未能善意和依据公平交易的合理标准行事的。

（c）知道披露该事实会纠正对方当事人关于证明或者体现全部或部分协议的书面文件的内容或者效力的错误的。

（d）由于双方存在信托或者信任关系，对方有权知道这一事实的。

§ 162. When a Misrepresentation Is Fraudulent or Material

（1）A misrepresentation is fraudulent if the maker intends his assertion to induce a party to manifest his assent and the maker

（a）knows or believes that the assertion is not in accord with the facts, or

（b）does not have the confidence that he states or implies in the truth of the assertion, or

（c）knows that he does not have the basis that he states or implies for the assertion.

（2）A misrepresentation is material if it would be likely to induce a reasonable person to manifest his assent, or if the maker knows that it would be likely to induce the recipient to do so.

第162条　何时误述具有欺诈性或者重大性

（1）误述人意图通过断言诱使当事人作出同意表示且误述人具有下列情

形的，误述具有欺诈性：

（a）知道或者相信断言与事实不符的，或者

（b）对断言的真实性并没有自己所说的或者暗示的信心的，或者

（c）知道断言并没有自己所说的或者暗示的基础的。

（2）可能会诱使理性常人[1]作出同意表示的，或者误述人知道可能会诱使相对人作出同意表示的，误述具有重大性。

§ 163. When a Misrepresentation Prevents Formation of a Contract

If a misrepresentation as to the character or essential terms of a proposed contract induces conduct that appears to be manifestation of assent by one who neither knows nor has reasonable opportunity to know of the character or essential terms of the proposed contract, his conduct is not effective as a manifestation of assent.

第 163 条　何时误述阻却合同成立

既不知道也无合理机会知道所提议合同的特点或者基本条款的人，由于受到关于该合同特点或者基本条款的误述的诱使，因而作出表面同意表示的行为的，该行为不是有效的同意表示。

§ 164. When a Misrepresentation Makes a Contract Voidable

（1）If a party's manifestation of assent is induced by either a fraudulent or a material misrepresentation by the other party upon which the recipient is justified in relying, the contract is voidable by the recipient.

（2）If a party's manifestation of assent is induced by either a fraudulent or a material misrepresentation by one who is not a party to the transaction upon which the recipient is justified in relying, the contract is voidable by the recipient, unless the

---

[1]　理性常人（reasonable person），reasonable person 的常见译法有"理性人""通情达理的人""普通正常人"等。译者认为后两个译名是正确的，但"理性人"的含义似乎重于 reasonable person。受张法连（2014）启发，并结合本文风格，在本文语境中译为"理性常人"。该词的内涵与译名参见张法连（2014）及薛波（2003）。

other party to the transaction in good faith and without reason to know of the misrepresentation either gives value or relies materially on the transaction.

第 164 条　何时误述使得合同可撤销

（1）当事人作出同意表示是由于受对方当事人欺诈性或者重大性误述的诱使，且当事人的信赖是合理的，则当事人可以撤销合同。

（2）当事人作出同意表示是由于受非交易当事人的欺诈性或者重大性误述的诱使，且当事人的信赖是合理的，则当事人可以撤销合同，但交易对方当事人在善意且无理由知道误述的情况下支付了对价或者对交易产生了实质信赖的情形除外。

§ 165. Cure by Change of Circumstances

If a contract is voidable because of a misrepresentation and, before notice of an intention to avoid the contract, the facts come into accord with the assertion, the contract is no longer voidable unless the recipient has been harmed by relying on the misrepresentation.

第 165 条　情形改变形成补救

因误述而可以撤销的合同，在通知撤销合同之前事实已经发生改变并与断言相符的，不再可以撤销，但误述相对人因信赖误述而已经受害的除外。

§ 166. When a Misrepresentation as to a Writing Justifies Reformation

If a party's manifestation of assent is induced by the other party's fraudulent misrepresentation as to the contents or effect of a writing evidencing or embodying in whole or in part an agreement, the court at the request of the recipient may reform the writing to express the terms of the agreement as asserted,

（a）if the recipient was justified in relying on the misrepresentation, and

（b）except to the extent that rights of third parties such as good faith purchasers for value will be unfairly affected.

第 166 条 何时有关书面文件的误述使得重订合理

当事人作出同意表示，是由于受对方当事人对证明或者体现全部或部分协议的书面文件的内容或者效力作出欺诈性误述的诱使，且有下列情形的，法院可以应误述相对人的要求重订书面协议，以表达所主张的协议条款：

（a）误述相对人对误述产生信赖是合理的，且

（b）诸如善意已付对价买受人的第三人的权利不会受到不公平影响的。

§ 167. When a Misrepresentation Is an Inducing Cause

A misrepresentation induces a party's manifestation of assent if it substantially contributes to his decision to manifest his assent.

第 167 条 何时误述成为诱使原因

误述实质性地帮助当事人作出同意表示决定的，属于诱使同意表示。

§ 168. Reliance on Assertions of Opinion

（1）An assertion is one of opinion if it expresses only a belief, without certainty, as to the existence of a fact or expresses only a judgment as to quality, value, authenticity, or similar matters.

（2）If it is reasonable to do so, the recipient of an assertion of a person's opinion as to facts not disclosed and not otherwise known to the recipient may properly interpret it as an assertion

（a）that the facts known to that person are not incompatible with his opinion, or

（b）that he knows facts sufficient to justify him in forming it.

第 168 条 信赖意见断言

（1）只是表达关于事实是否存在的不确定看法的，或者只是表达对质量、价值、真实性或者类似问题的判断的，是意见断言。

（2）如果合理，相对人可以适宜地将关于未向自己披露、自己也未从其他方面获知的事实的意见断言解释如下：

（a）断言人所知的事实与其意见不是相互矛盾的，或者

（b）断言人所知的事实足以使其合理地作出断言。

§ 169. When Reliance on an Assertion of Opinion Is Not Justified

To the extent that an assertion is one of opinion only, the recipient is not justified in relying on it unless the recipient

（a）stands in such a relation of trust and confidence to the person whose opinion is asserted that the recipient is reasonable in relying on it, or

（b）reasonably believes that, as compared with himself, the person whose opinion is asserted has special skill, judgment or objectivity with respect to the subject matter, or

（c）is for some other special reason particularly susceptible to a misrepresentation of the type involved.

第 169 条　何时信赖意见断言不当

除下列情形以外，相对人信赖仅仅是表达意见的断言是不当的：

（a）相对人与意见断言人具有信赖和亲密关系，因而产生信赖是合理的，或者

（b）相对人合理地认为，与自己相比，意见断言人具有与标的有关的特殊技能、判断或者客观性的，或者

（c）由于其他特殊原因，相对人尤其易于受到此类误述影响的。

§ 170. Reliance on Assertions as to Matters of Law

If an assertion is one as to a matter of law, the same rules that apply in the case of other assertions determine whether the recipient is justified in relying on it.

第 170 条　信赖法律问题断言

断言是有关法律问题的，由适用于其他断言的规则确定相对人的信赖是否合理。

§ 171. When Reliance on an Assertion of Intention Is Not Justified

（1）To the extent that an assertion is one of intention only, the recipient is not justified in relying on it if in the circumstances a misrepresentation of intention is consistent with reasonable standards of dealing.

（2）If it is reasonable to do so, the promisee may properly interpret a promise as an assertion that the promisor intends to perform the promise.

第 171 条　何时信赖意图断言不当

（1）断言仅仅是表述意图的，如果具体情形下的意图误述符合合理的交易标准，则相对人产生信赖是不合理的。

（2）如果合理，受诺人可以适宜地将允诺解释为允诺人意图履行允诺的断言。

§ 172. When Fault Makes Reliance Unjustified

A recipient's fault in not knowing or discovering the facts before making the contract does not make his reliance unjustified unless it amounts to a failure to act in good faith and in accordance with reasonable standards of fair dealing.

第 172 条　何时过错使得信赖不当

相对人在订立合同之前不知道或者未能发现事实真相的，这一过错并不使得其信赖缺乏合理性，但过错构成未能善意且依照公平交易的合理标准行事的除外。

§ 173. When Abuse of Fiduciary Relation Makes a Contract Voidable

If a fiduciary makes a contract with his beneficiary relating to matters within the scope of the fiduciary relation, the contract is voidable by the beneficiary, unless

（a）it is on fair terms, and

（b）all parties beneficially interested manifest assent with full understanding of their legal rights and of all relevant facts that the fiduciary knows or should know.

第 173 条　何时滥用信托关系使得合同可撤销

除下列情形以外，受托人就信托关系范围内的事项与受益人订立合同的，受益人可以撤销合同：

（a）合同条款公平的，且

（b）所有具有受益利益的当事人，是在完全了解自己的法定权利以及受托人知道或者应当知道的一切相关事实后作出同意表示的。

TOPIC 2. DURESS AND UNDUE INFLUENCE
第二节　胁迫与不当影响

§ 174. When Duress by Physical Compulsion Prevents Formation of a Contract

If conduct that appears to be a manifestation of assent by a party who does not intend to engage in that conduct is physically compelled by duress, the conduct is not effective as a manifestation of assent.

第 174 条　何时通过人身强制进行胁迫阻却合同成立

当事人没有意图实施某行为，而是由于受到人身强制的胁迫作出表面同意表示的行为的，该行为不是有效的同意表示。

§ 175. When Duress by Threat Makes a Contract Voidable

（1）If a party's manifestation of assent is induced by an improper threat by the other party that leaves the victim no reasonable alternative, the contract is voidable by the victim.

（2）If a party's manifestation of assent is induced by one who is not a party to the transaction, the contract is voidable by the victim unless the other party to the transaction in good faith and without reason to know of the duress either gives value or relies materially on the transaction.

第 175 条　何时通过威胁进行胁迫使得合同可撤销

（1）当事人作出同意表示是由于受到对方当事人不当威胁的诱使，因而别无合理选择的，受害人可以撤销合同。

（2）当事人作出同意表示是由于受非交易当事人的诱使的，受害人可以撤销合同，但交易对方当事人在善意且无理由知道胁迫的情况下支付了对价或者对交易产生了实质信赖的除外。

§ 176. When a Threat Is Improper

（1）A threat is improper if

（a）what is threatened is a crime or a tort, or the threat itself would be a crime or a tort if it resulted in obtaining property,

（b）what is threatened is a criminal prosecution,

（c）what is threatened is the use of civil process and the threat is made in bad faith, or

（d）the threat is a breach of the duty of good faith and fair dealing under a contract with the recipient.

（2）A threat is improper if the resulting exchange is not on fair terms, and

（a）the threatened act would harm the recipient and would not significantly benefit the party making the threat,

（b）the effectiveness of the threat in inducing the manifestation of assent is significantly increased by prior unfair dealing by the party making the threat, or

（c）what is threatened is otherwise a use of power for illegitimate ends.

第 176 条　何时威胁是不适当的

（1）有下列情形的威胁是不适当的：

（a）用以威胁的是犯罪或者侵权行为，或者威胁本身如果取得财产将会构成犯罪或者侵权行为的，

（b）用以威胁的是刑事诉讼的，

（c）用以威胁的是实施民事诉讼程序且威胁是恶意作出的，或者

（d）威胁行为违反了与相对人订立的合同中规定的善意与公平交易义务的。

（2）产生了条款不公平的交换且具有下列情形时，威胁是不适当的：

（a）用以威胁的行为将会危害相对方且不会显著使威胁方受益的，

（b）由于威胁方先前的不公平交易，威胁的效果在诱使同意表示的作出方面显著增加的，或者

（c）用以威胁的是在其他方面利用权力达到非法目的的。

§ 177. When Undue Influence Makes a Contract Voidable

（1）Undue influence is unfair persuasion of a party who is under the domination of the person exercising the persuasion or who by virtue of the relation between them is justified in assuming that that person will not act in a manner inconsistent with his welfare.

（2）If a party's manifestation of assent is induced by undue influence by the other party, the contract is voidable by the victim.

（3）If a party's manifestation of assent is induced by one who is not a party to the transaction, the contract is voidable by the victim unless the other party to the transaction in good faith and without reason to know of the undue influence either gives value or relies materially on the transaction.

第 177 条　何时不当影响使得合同可撤销

（1）不当影响，是指对处于劝导人主导之下的，或者由于双方之间的关系而合理地认为劝导人的行为不会与自己的利益不相一致的合同当事人的不公平劝导。

（2）当事人作出同意表示是由于受对方当事人不当影响的诱使的，受害人可以撤销合同。

（3）当事人作出同意表示是由于受非交易当事人的诱使的，受害人可以撤销合同，但交易对方当事人在善意且无理由知道不当影响的情况下支付了对价或者对交易产生了实质信赖的除外。

第八章

因违反公共政策而
不可强制执行

Chapter 8
UNENFORCEABILITY ON
GROUNDS OF PUBLIC POLICY

TOPIC 1. UNENFORCEABILITY IN GENERAL
第一节　不可强制执行的一般规则

§ 178. When a Term Is Unenforceable on Grounds of Public Policy

（1）A promise or other term of an agreement is unenforceable on grounds of public policy if legislation provides that it is enforceable or the interest in its enforcement is clearly outweighed in the circumstances by a public policy against the enforcement of such terms.

（2）In weighing the interest in the enforcement of a term, account is taken of

（a）the parties' justified expectations,

（b）any forfeiture that would result if enforcement were denied, and

（c）any special public interest in the enforcement of the particular term.

（3）In weighing a public policy against enforcement of a term, account is taken of

（a）the strength of that policy as manifested by legislation or judicial decisions,

（b）the likelihood that a refusal to enforce the term will further that policy,

（c）the seriousness of any misconduct involved and the extent to which it was deliberate, and

（d）the directness of the connection between that misconduct and the term.

第 178 条　何时合同条款因违反公共政策不可强制执行

（1）立法规定不可强制执行的，或者强制执行的利益在具体情形中明显低于禁止强制执行此种条款的公共政策的，允诺或者协议的其他条款因违反公共政策不可强制执行。

（2）衡量条款的强制执行利益时，所考虑因素包括：

（a）当事人的合理期待，

（b）拒绝强制执行会产生的没收，以及

（c）强制执行特定条款具有的特殊公共利益。

（3）衡量禁止条款执行的公共政策时，所考虑因素包括：

（a）立法或者司法判决所表现的公共政策的力度，

（b）拒绝强制执行条款促进政策的可能性，

（c）所涉不当行为的严重性以及行为的故意程度，以及

（d）不当行为与条款关联的直接性。

§ 179. Bases of Public Policies against Enforcement

A policy against the enforcement of promises or other terms may be derived by the court from

（a）legislation relevant to such a policy, or

（b）the need to protect some aspect of the public welfare, as is the case for the judicial policies against, for example,

（i）restraint of trade（§§ 186−188），

（ii）impairment of family relations（§§ 189−191）, and

（iii）interference with other protected interests（§§ 192−196, 356）.

第 179 条　禁止强制执行的公共政策基础

法院可以从以下方面发展禁止强制执行允诺或者其他条款的公共政策：

（a）与该政策有关的立法，或者

（b）保护某方面公共福利的需要，例如司法政策对诸如下列情形的禁止：

（i）限制贸易（第 186~188 条），

（ii）损害家庭关系（第 189~191 条），以及

（iii）干预其他受保护的权益（第 192~196 条，第 356 条）。

§ 180. Effect of Excusable Ignorance

If a promisee is excusably ignorant of facts or of legislation of a minor character, of which the promisor is not excusably ignorant and in the absence of which the promise would be enforceable, the promisee has a claim for damages for its breach but cannot recover damages for anything that he has done after he learns of the facts or legislation.

第 180 条　情有可原的不知情的效力

受诺人对事实或者对次要性质的立法并不知情且情有可原，而对此允诺人并不存在情有可原的不知情，且这些事实或者立法若不存在允诺将是可以强制执行的，受诺人有权请求违约损害赔偿，但了解该事实或者立法之后所做之事不能获得损害赔偿。

§ 181. Effect of Failure to Comply with Licensing or Similar Requirement

If a party is prohibited from doing an act because of his failure to comply with a licensing, registration or similar requirement, a promise in consideration of his doing the act or of his promise to do it is unenforceable on grounds of public policy if

(a) the requirement has a regulatory purpose, and

(b) the interest in the enforcement of the promise is clearly outweighed by the public policy behind the requirement.

第 181 条　未遵守许可或者类似要求的效力

当事人由于未能满足许可、注册或者类似要求而被禁止从事某行为的，以其实施该行为或者允诺实施该行为为对价的允诺，在下列情形下因违反公共政策而不可强制执行：

（a）要求具有规范性目的，且
（b）强制执行允诺的利益明显低于要求背后的公共政策。

§ 182. Effect of Performance if Intended Use Is Improper

If the promisee has substantially performed, enforcement of a promise is not precluded on grounds of public policy because of some improper use that the promisor intends to make of what he obtains unless the promisee

(a) acted for the purpose of furthering the improper use, or

(b) knew of the use and the use involves grave social harm.

第 182 条　意图不正当使用时的履行效力

受诺人已经实质性地履行了允诺的，不因允诺人意图不正当地使用其所得而使得允诺因违反公共政策而不可强制执行，但受诺人有下列情形的除外：

（a）为了促进允诺人的不正当使用而行事的，或者

（b）事先了解允诺人的使用，且该使用涉及对社会的严重损害的。

§ 183. When Agreement Is Enforceable as to Agreed Equivalents

If the parties' performances can be apportioned into corresponding pairs of part performances so that the parts of each pair are properly regarded as agreed equivalents and one pair is not offensive to public policy, that portion of the agreement is enforceable by a party who did not engage in serious misconduct.

第 183 条　何时可以就约定的对等履行强制执行协议

合同当事人的履行可以划分为多个对应的部分履行的组合，每个组合中的对应部分可以适宜地视为约定的对等履行，且有一个组合没有违反公共政策的，协议的该部分可以由没有实施严重不当行为的当事人强制执行。

§ 184. When Rest of Agreement Is Enforceable

（1）If less than all of an agreement is unenforceable under the rule stated in § 178, a court may nevertheless enforce the rest of the agreement in favor of a party who did not engage in serious misconduct if the performance as to which the agreement is unenforceable is not an essential part of the agreed exchange.

（2）A court may treat only part of a term as unenforceable under the rule stated in Subsection（1）if the party who seeks to enforce the term obtained it in good faith and in accordance with reasonable standards of fair dealing.

第 184 条　何时协议的剩余部分可以强制执行

（1）协议并非全部是第 178 条所述规则规定的不可强制执行条款的，如果协议不可强制执行部分的履行不是约定交换的本质部分，法院仍然可以为

没有实施严重不当行为的当事人的利益而强制执行协议的剩余部分。

（2）请求强制执行合同条款的当事人善意且依照公平交易的合理标准订立该条款的，法院可以按照第（1）项的规定认定该条款只有部分不可强制执行。

§ 185. Excuse of a Condition on Grounds of Public Policy

To the extent that a term requiring the occurrence of a condition is unenforceable under the rule stated in § 178, a court may excuse the non-occurrence of the condition unless its occurrence was an essential part of the agreed exchange.

第 185 条　以公共政策为由对条件免责

要求条件成就的条款根据第 178 条所述规则的规定不可强制执行的，法院可以对条件的不成就免责，但条件成就是所达成交换的本质部分的情形除外。

TOPIC 2. RESTRAINT OF TRADE
第二节　限制贸易

§ 186. Promise in Restraint of Trade

（1）A promise is unenforceable on grounds of public policy if it is unreasonably in restraint of trade.

（2）A promise is in restraint of trade if its performance would limit competition in any business or restrict the promisor in the exercise of a gainful occupation.

第 186 条　限制贸易的允诺

（1）不合理地限制贸易的允诺因违反公共政策而不可强制执行。

（2）允诺的履行将会限制任一商业领域的竞争，或者限制允诺人的营利性职业（工作）的，是对贸易的限制。

§ 187. Non-Ancillary Restraints on Competition

A promise to refrain from competition that imposes a restraint that is not ancillary to an otherwise valid transaction or relationship is unreasonably in restraint of trade.

第 187 条　非附属性限制竞争

不予竞争的允诺形成了对竞争的限制，且限制并非附属于其他方面都有效的交易或者关系的，是对贸易不合理的限制。

§ 188. Ancillary Restraints on Competition

（1）A promise to refrain from competition that imposes a restraint that is ancillary to an otherwise valid transaction or relationship is unreasonably in restraint of trade if

（a）the restraint is greater than is needed to protect the promisee's legitimate interest, or

（b）the promisee's need is outweighed by the hardship to the promisor and the likely injury to the public.

（2）Promises imposing restraints that are ancillary to a valid transaction or relationship include the following:

（a）a promise by the seller of a business not to compete with the buyer in such a way as to injury the value of the business sold;

（b）a promise by an employee or other agent not to compete with his employer or other principal;

（c）a promise by a partner not to compete with the partnership.

第 188 条　对竞争的附属性限制

（1）不予竞争的允诺形成的限制附属于其他方面都有效的交易或者关系的，在下列情形下不合理地限制了贸易：

（a）限制超过了保护受诺人合法权益所需的，或者

（b）受诺人所需低于带给允诺人的困难和对公众可能造成的损害的。

（2）形成附属于有效交易或者关系的限制的允诺包括：

（a）交易卖方不以有损于所售交易价值的方式与买方竞争的允诺；

（b）雇员或者其他代理人不与雇主或者其他被代理人竞争的允诺；

（c）合伙人不与合伙组织竞争的允诺。

TOPIC 3. IMPAIRMENT OF FAMILY RELATIONS
第三节　损害家庭关系

§ 189. Promise in Restraint of Marriage

A promise is unenforceable on grounds of public policy if it is unreasonably in restraint of marriage.

第 189 条　限制婚姻的允诺

不合理地限制婚姻的允诺因违反公共政策而不可强制执行。

§ 190. Promise Detrimental to Marital Relationship

（1）A promise by a person contemplating marriage or by a married person, other than as part of an enforceable separation agreement, is unenforceable on grounds of public policy if it would change some essential incident of the marital relationship in a way detrimental to the public interest in the marriage relationship. A separation agreement is unenforceable on grounds of public policy unless it is made after separation or in contemplation of an immediate separation and is fair in the circumstances.

（2）A promise that tends unreasonably to encourage divorce or separation is unenforceable on grounds of public policy.

第 190 条　损害婚姻关系的允诺

（1）考虑结婚或者已经结婚的人作出的允诺，除作为可强制执行的分居协议中的部分内容以外，会以有损于婚姻关系中的公共利益的方式改变婚姻关系的某些本质性附属内容的，因违反公共政策而不可强制执行。分居协议因违反公共政策而不可强制执行，但在分居之后订立，或者订立时考虑马上分居且在当时情形下是公平的除外。

（2）容易不合理地鼓励离婚或者分居的允诺因违反公共政策而不可强制执行。

§ 191. Promise Affecting Custody

A promise affecting the right of custody of a minor child is unenforceable on grounds of public policy unless the disposition as to custody is consistent with the best interest of the child.

第 191 条　影响监护的允诺

影响对未成年子女的监护权的允诺因违反公共政策而不可强制执行，但有关监护的安排与子女的最大利益相一致的除外。

TOPIC 4. INTERFERENCE WITH OTHER PROTECTED INTERESTS
第四节　干预其他受保护权益

§ 192. Promise Involving Commission of a Tort

A promise to commit a tort or to induce the commission of a tort is unenforceable on grounds of public policy.

第 192 条　涉及实施侵权的允诺

实施侵权行为或者诱使侵权实施的允诺因违反公共政策而不可强制执行。

§ 193. Promise Inducing Violation of Fiduciary Duty

A promise by a fiduciary to violate his fiduciary duty or a promise that tends to induce such a violation is unenforceable on grounds of public policy.

第 193 条 诱使违反信托义务的允诺

受托人作出的违反信托义务的允诺，或者容易诱使违反信托义务发生的允诺，因违反公共政策而不可强制执行。

§ 194. Promise Interfering with Contract with Another

A promise that tortiously interferes with performance of a contract with a third person or a tortiously induced promise to commit a breach of contract is unenforceable on grounds of public policy.

第 194 条 干预他人合同的允诺

以侵权方式干预与第三人的合同履行的允诺，或者受到侵权诱使作出的违反合同的允诺，因违反公共政策而不可强制执行。

§ 195. Term Exempting from Liability for Harm Caused Intentionally, Recklessly or Negligently

（1）A term exempting a party from tort liability for harm caused intentionally or recklessly is unenforceable on grounds of public policy.

（2）A term exempting a party from tort liability for harm caused negligently is unenforceable on grounds of public policy if

（a）the term exempts an employer from liability to an employee for injury in the course of his employment;

（b）the term exempts one charged with a duty of public service from liability to one to whom that duty is owed for compensation for breach of that duty, or

（c）the other party is similarly a member of a class protected against the class to which the first party belongs.

（3）A term exempting a seller of a product from his special tort liability for physical harm to a user or consumer is unenforceable on grounds of public policy unless the term is fairly bargained for and is consistent with the policy underlying that liability.

第 195 条　免除因故意、极度轻率或者过失造成的损害的条款

（1）免除当事人因故意或者极度轻率造成损害而承担的侵权责任的条款，因违反公共政策而不可强制执行。

（2）免除当事人因过失造成损害而承担的侵权责任的条款，有下列情形的，因违反公共政策而不可强制执行：

（a）免除了雇员在雇佣期间所遭受伤害的雇主责任的；

（b）免除了负有公共服务义务的人因违反其义务而应向相对人承担的赔偿责任的，或者

（c）对方当事人类似于受保护群体的成员，前者当事人属于相对群体的成员的。

（3）免除产品销售者对用户或者消费者所遭受的身体伤害承担特殊侵权责任的条款，因违反公共政策而不可强制执行，但条款是公平交易的对象且与责任背后的公共政策一致的除外。

§ 196. Term Exempting from Consequences of Misrepresentation

A term unreasonably exempting a party from the legal consequences of a misrepresentation is unenforceable on grounds of public policy.

第 196 条　免除误述后果的条款

不合理地免除当事人因误述而承担的法律后果的条款，因违反公共政策而不可强制执行。

TOPIC 5. RESTITUTION
第五节 返还

§ 197. Restitution Generally Unavailable

Except as stated in §§ 198 and 199, a party has no claim in restitution for performance that he has rendered under or in return for a promise that is unenforceable on grounds of public policy unless denial of restitution would cause disproportionate forfeiture.

第197条 一般不予返还

除了第198条和第199条所述规则以外,当事人根据或者为回报因违反公共政策而不可强制执行的允诺而给付的履行,无权请求返还,但不予返还会造成不成比例的没收的除外。

§ 198. Restitution in Favor of Party Who Is Excusably Ignorant or Is Not Equally in the Wrong

A party has a claim in restitution for performance that he has rendered under or in return for a promise that is unenforceable on grounds of public policy if

(a) he was excusably ignorant of the facts or of legislation of a minor character, in the absence of which the promise would be enforceable, or

(b) he was not equally in the wrong with the promisor.

第198条 有利于不知情但情有可原或者过错程度较轻的当事人的返还

当事人根据或者为回报因违反公共政策而不可强制执行的允诺而给付的履行,有下列情形的,有权请求返还:

(a) 当事人对事实或者次要性的立法不知情且情有可原,且若非这些事实或者立法允诺将可以强制执行的,或者

(b) 与允诺人相比,当事人的过错程度较轻的。

§ 199. Restitution Where Party Withdraws or Situation Is Contrary to Public Interest

A party has a claim in restitution for performance that he has rendered under or in return for a promise that is unenforceable on grounds of public policy if he did not engage in serious misconduct and

（a）he withdraws from the transaction before the improper purpose has been achieved, or

（b）allowance of the claim would put an end to a continuing situation that is contrary to the public interest.

第 199 条　当事人退出交易或者情形与公共利益相悖时的返还

对于当事人遵照因违反公共政策而不可强制执行的允诺给付的履行，或者为交换因违反公共政策而不可强制执行的允诺而给付的履行，当事人没有实施严重不法行为且有下列情形的，有权请求返还：

（a）实现不正当目的之前退出交易的，或者

（b）允许返还将会结束与公共利益相悖情形的持续的。

第九章

合同义务的范围

Chapter 9
THE SCOPE OF CONTRACTUAL
OBLIGATIONS

TOPIC 1. THE MEANING OF AGREEMENTS
第一节　协议的意义

§ 200. Interpretation of Promise or Agreement

Interpretation of a promise or agreement or a term thereof is the ascertainment of its meaning.

第 200 条　允诺或者协议的解释

允诺、协议或者其条款的解释，是对其意义的确定。

§ 201. Whose Meaning Prevails

（1）Where the parties have attached the same meaning to a promise or agreement or a term thereof, it is interpreted in accordance with that meaning.

（2）Where the parties have attached different meanings to a promise or agreement or a term thereof, it is interpreted in accordance with the meaning attached by one of them if at the time the agreement was made

（a）that party did not know of any different meaning attached by the other, and the other knew the meaning attached by the first party; or

（b）that party had no reason to know of any different meaning attached by the other, and the other had reason to know the meaning attached by the first party.

（3）Except as stated in this Section, neither party is bound by the meaning attached by the other, even though the result may be a failure of mutual assent.

第 201 条　以谁的意义为准

（1）当事人对允诺、协议或者其条款赋予了相同意义的，依照该意义进行解释。

（2）当事人对允诺、协议或者其条款赋予了不同意义的，如果协议达成之时有下列情形，则依照一方当事人所赋予的意义进行解释：

（a）该当事人不知道对方赋予的任何不同意义，而对方知道前者当事人所赋予的意义的；或者

（b）该当事人没有理由知道对方赋予的任何不同意义，而对方有理由知道前者当事人所赋予的意义的。

（3）除本条所述规则以外，任何一方不受对方所赋予意义的约束，尽管结果可能是不存在相互同意。

§ 202. Rules in Aid of Interpretation

（1）Words and other conduct are interpreted in the light of all the circumstances, and if the principal purpose of the parties is ascertainable it is given great weight.

（2）A writing is interpreted as a whole, and all writings that are part of the same transaction are interpreted together.

（3）Unless a different intention is manifested,

（a）where language has a generally prevailing meaning, it is interpreted in accordance with that meaning;

（b）technical terms and words of art are given their technical meaning when used in a transaction within their technical field.

（4）Where an agreement involves repeated occasions for performance by either party with knowledge of the nature of the performance and opportunity for objection to it by the other, any course of performance accepted or acquiesced in without objection is given great weight in the interpretation of the agreement.

（5）Wherever reasonable, the manifestations of intention of the parties to a promise or agreement are interpreted as consistent with each other and with any relevant course of performance, course of dealing, or usage of trade.

第 202 条 解释的辅助规则

（1）语词或者其他行为根据情形进行解释，且当事人的主要目的能确定

的，主要目的占有重要地位。

（2）书面文件作为整体进行解释，构成同一交易的所有书面文件一并进行解释。

（3）除有不同的意思表示以外，

（a）语言有通用的优先意义的，依照该意义解释。

（b）技术术语或者专用语词在其所属技术领域的交易中使用的，赋予其技术意义。

（4）协议涉及任意一方当事人重复履行，且对方知晓履行性质并有反对机会的，所接受的或者没有反对而默许的任何履行历史，在协议解释时占有重要地位。

（5）在合理情况下，允诺或者协议当事人的意思表示解释为相互一致，并与任何相关的履行历史、交易历史或者行业惯例相一致。

§ 203. Standards of Preference in Interpretation

In the interpretation of a promise or agreement or a term thereof, the following standards of preference are generally applicable：

（a）an interpretation which gives a reasonable, lawful, and effective meaning to all the terms is preferred to an interpretation which leaves a part unreasonable, unlawful, or of no effect；

（b）express terms are given greater weight than course of performance, course of dealing, and usage of trade, course of performance is given greater weight than course of dealing or usage of trade, and course of dealing is given greater weight than usage of trade；

（c）specific terms and exact terms are given greater weight than general language；

（d）separately negotiated or added terms are given greater weight than standardized terms or other terms not separately negotiated.

第 203 条　解释的优先标准

解释允诺、协议或者其条款时，通常适用下列优先标准：

（a）赋予全体条款合理、合法、有效意义的解释，优先于导致部分条款不合理、不合法或者无效的解释；

（b）明示条款的重要性大于履行历史、交易历史和行业惯例，履行历史的重要性大于交易历史或者行业惯例，交易历史的重要性大于行业惯例；

（c）具体条款和精准条款的重要性大于一般性语言；

（d）单独磋商的或者增加的条款的重要性大于标准化条款或者其他非单独磋商的条款。

§ 204. Supplying an Omitted Essential Term

When the parties to a bargain sufficiently defined to be a contract have not a-greed with respect to a term which is essential to a determination of their rights and duties, a term which is reasonable in the circumstances is supplied by the court.

第 204 条　补充被省略的基本条款

当事人的交易可以充分认定为合同，但当事人尚未就确定权利义务所必须的某条款达成一致的，法院根据具体情形补充合理条款。

TOPIC 2.　CONSIDERATIONS OF FAIRNESS AND THE PUBLIC INTEREST
第二节　考虑公平与公共利益

§ 205. Duty of Good Faith and Fair Dealing

Every contract imposes upon each party a duty of good faith and fair dealing in its performance and its enforcement.

第 205 条　善意与公平交易义务

所有合同赋予各方当事人履行或者强制执行时的善意与公平交易义务。

§ 206.　Interpretation Against the Draftsman

In choosing among the reasonable meanings of a promise or agreement or a term thereof, that meaning is generally preferred which operates against the party who supplies the words or from whom a writing otherwise proceeds.

第 206 条 不利于合同起草方的解释

在允诺、协议或者其条款的数个合理解释之间进行选择时，不利于语词提供方或者其他方式的书面文件提供方的解释一般具有优先性。

§ 207. Interpretation Favoring the Public

In choosing among the reasonable meanings of a promise or agreement or a term thereof, a meaning that serves the public interest is generally preferred.

第 207 条 有利于公众的解释

在允诺、协议或者其条款的数个合理解释之间进行选择时，服务于公共利益的解释一般具有优先性。

§ 208. Unconscionable Contract or Term

If a contract or term thereof is unconscionable at the time the contract is made a court may refuse to enforce the contract, or may enforce the remainder of the contract without the unconscionable term, or may so limit the application of any unconscionable term as to avoid any unconscionable result.

第 208 条 显失公平的合同或者条款

合同或者合同条款在合同订立时显失公平的，法院可以拒绝强制执行合同，或者可以强制执行不含显失公平条款的部分，也可以限制任何显失公平条款的适用以避免任何显失公平结果的出现。

TOPIC 3. EFFECT OF ADOPTION OF A WRITING
第三节 采用书面形式的效力

§ 209. Integrated Agreements

（1）An integrated agreement is a writing or writings constituting a final expression of one or more terms of an agreement.

（2）Whether there is an integrated agreement is to be determined by the court as a question preliminary to determination of a question of interpretation or to application of the parol evidence rule.

（3）Where the parties reduce an agreement to a writing which in view of its completeness and specificity reasonably appears to be a complete agreement, it is taken to be an integrated agreement unless it is established by other evidence that the writing did not constitute a final expression.

第 209 条 完整协议

（1）完整协议，是指最终表述协议的一个或者多个条款的一份或者多份书面文件。

（2）是否存在完整协议，由法院将其作为解释问题之前或者适用口头证据规则之前的问题进行确定。

（3）当事人将协议落实为书面文件，且书面文件的完整性和具体性合理地显示为全部协议的，书面文件视为完整协议，但有其他证据证明书面文件没有构成最终表述的除外。

§ 210. Completely and Partially Integrated Agreements

（1）A completely integrated agreement is an integrated agreement adopted by the parties as a complete and exclusive statement of the terms of the agreement.

（2）A partially integrated agreement is an integrated agreement other than a completely integrated agreement.

（3）Whether an agreement is completely or partially integrated is to be deter-

mined by the court as a question preliminary to determination of a question of interpretation or to application of the parol evidence rule.

第 210 条　完全的与部分的完整协议

（1）完全完整协议，是指当事人用作协议条款的完全性、排他性表述的完整协议。

（2）部分完整协议，是指除完全的完整协议以外的完整协议。

（3）协议是完全的还是部分的完整协议，由法院作为确定所解释问题之前或者适用口头证据规则之前的问题进行确定。

§ 211. Standardized Agreements

（1）Except as stated in Subsection（3）, where a party to an agreement signs or
otherwise manifests assent to a writing and has reason to believe that like writings are
regularly used to embody terms of agreements of the same type, he adopts the writing
as an integrated agreement with respect to the terms included in the writing.

（2）Such a writing is interpreted wherever reasonable as treating alike all those
similarly situated, without regard to their knowledge or understanding of the standard
terms of the writing.

（3）Where the other party has reason to believe that the party manifesting such
assent would not do so if he knew that the writing contained a particular term, the
term is not part of the agreement.

第 211 条　标准化协议

（1）除第（3）款所述规则以外，协议当事人在书面文件上签字或者以其他方式作出了同意表示，并且有理由相信同样的书面文件经常用以表述相同类型的协议条款的，就所包括的条款而言，当事人采用了该书面文件作为完整的协议。

（2）在合理的情况下，此类书面文件解释为对相似情景中的人相同对待，无论他们是否知道或者理解书面文件的标准条款。

（3）对方当事人有理由认为，作出同意表示的当事人如果知道书面文件包含特定条款就不会表示同意的，那么该条款不是协议的组成部分。

§ 212. Interpretation of Integrated Agreement

（1）The interpretation of an integrated agreement is directed to the meaning of the terms of the writing or writings in the light of the circumstances, in accordance with the rules stated in this Chapter.

（2）A question of interpretation of an integrated agreement is to be determined by the trier of fact if it depends on the credibility of extrinsic evidence or on a choice among reasonable inferences to be drawn from extrinsic evidence. Otherwise a question of interpretation of an integrated agreement is to be determined as a question of law.

第 212 条　完整协议的解释

（1）完整协议的解释，是按照本章所述规则并结合具体情形解释一份或者多份书面文件的条款意义。

（2）完整协议的解释问题依赖于外部证据的可信度，或者依赖于在根据外部证据作出的合理推论中进行选择的，由审理事实者确定。其他情况下，完整协议的解释问题作为法律问题确定。

§ 213. Effect of Integrated Agreement on Prior Agreements (Parol Evidence Rule)

（1）A binding integrated agreement discharges prior agreements to the extent that it is inconsistent with them.

（2）A binding completely integrated agreement discharges prior agreements to the extent that they are within its scope.

（3）An integrated agreement that is not binding or that is voidable and avoided does not discharge a prior agreement. But an integrated agreement, even though not binding, may be effective to render inoperative a term which would have been part of the agreement if it had not been integrated.

第213条　完整协议对于先前协议的效力（口头证据规则）

（1）有约束力的完整协议在与其不一致的范围内解除先前协议。

（2）有约束力的完全完整协议在其覆盖范围内解除先前协议。

（3）不具有约束力的或者可撤销并已经撤销的完整协议不解除先前协议。但即使不具有约束力，完整协议也可能使若非并入完整协议将是协议组成部分的条款无法产生效力。

§ 214. Evidence of Prior or Contemporaneous Agreements and Negotiations

Agreements and negotiations prior to or contemporaneous with the adoption of a writing are admissible in evidence to establish

（a）that the writing is or is not an integrated agreement；

（b）that the integrated agreement, if any, is completely or partially integrated；

（c）the meaning of the writing, whether or not integrated；

（d）illegality, fraud, duress, mistake, lack of consideration, or other invalidating cause；

（e）ground for granting or denying rescission, reformation, specific performance, or other remedy.

第214条　先前或者同时的协议与磋商作为证据

采用书面文件之前或者与此同时的协议与磋商，可以用作证明下列事项的证据：

（a）书面文件是否是完整协议；

（b）如果存在完整协议，是完全完整协议还是部分完整协议；

（c）无论是否是完整协议，书面文件的意义是什么；

（d）非法、欺诈、胁迫、错误、缺乏对价或者其他无效事由；

（e）准予或者驳回解约、重订、具体履行或者其他救济的理由。

§ 215. Contradiction of Integrated Terms

Except as stated in the preceding Section, where there is a binding agreement, either completely or partially integrated, evidence of prior or contemporaneous agreements or negotiations is not admissible in evidence to contradict a term of the writing.

第 215 条　与完整协议条款冲突

除前条所述规则以外，存在有约束力的完全完整协议或者部分完整协议的，证明先前或同时协议或者磋商的证据不能用作否定书面文件条款的证据。

§ 216. Consistent Additional Terms

(1) Evidence of a consistent additional term is admissible to supplement an integrated agreement unless the court finds that the agreement was completely integrated.

(2) An agreement is not completely integrated if the writing omits a consistent additional agreed term which is

(a) agreed to for separate consideration, or

(b) such a term as in the circumstances might naturally be omitted from the writing.

第 216 条　一致的附加条款

(1) 证明一致的附加条款的证据可以用于补充完整协议，但法院认定协议是完全完整协议的除外。

(2) 书面文件省略了达成一致的附加条款，且该附加条款有下列情形的，协议不是完全完整协议：

(a) 为了单独的对价而达成的，或者

(b) 在当时的情形下，此类条款或许会自然从书面文件中省略的。

§ 217. Integrated Agreement Subject to Oral Requirement of a Condition

Where the parties to a written agreement agree orally that performance of the agreement is subject to the occurrence of a stated condition, the agreement is not integrated with respect to the oral condition.

第 217 条　必须符合口头要求的条件的完整协议

书面协议的当事人口头约定，协议的履行取决于所述条件的成就的，该协议就口头条件而言不是完整协议。

§ 218. Untrue Recitals; Evidence of Consideration

(1) A recital of a fact in an integrated agreement may be shown to be untrue.

(2) Evidence is admissible to prove whether or not there is consideration for a promise, even though the parties have reduced their agreement to a writing which appears to be a completely integrated agreement.

第 218 条　不真实的陈述；对价的证据

(1) 完整协议中的事实陈述可能被证明是不真实的。

(2) 即使当事人已将协议制作成形式上是完全完整协议的书面文件，也可以采信证明允诺是否存在对价的证据。

TOPIC 4. SCOPE AS AFFECTED BY USAGE
第四节　受惯例影响的范围

§ 219. Usage

Usage is habitual or customary practice.

第 219 条　惯例

惯例，是指习惯性的或者惯常性的做法。

§ 220. Usage Relevant to Interpretation

(1) An agreement is interpreted in accordance with a relevant usage if each party knew or had reason to know of the usage and neither party knew or had reason to know that the meaning attached by the other was inconsistent with the usage.

(2) When the meaning attached by one party accorded with a relevant usage and the other knew or had reason to know of the usage, the other is treated as having known or had reason to know the meaning attached by the first party.

第 220 条　与解释有关的惯例

（1）各方当事人都知道或者有理由知道某个相关惯例，并且都不知道或者没有合理理由知道对方所赋予的意义是与惯例不一致的，依据该惯例解释协议。

（2）一方当事人所赋予的意义与某个相关惯例一致，并且对方知道或者有理由知道该惯例的，视为对方已经知道或者有理由知道前者当事人所赋予的意义。

§ 221. Usage Supplementing an Agreement

An agreement is supplemented or qualified by a reasonable usage with respect to agreements of the same type if each party knows or has reason to know of the usage and neither party knows or has reason to know that the other party has an intention inconsistent with the usage.

第 221 条　补充协议的惯例

各方当事人都知道或者有理由知道同类协议的某个合理惯例，并且都不知道或没有合理理由知道对方当事人的意图与该惯例不一致的，协议受该惯例的补充或者限制。

§ 222.　Usage of Trade

（1）A usage of trade is a usage having such regularity of observance in a place, vocation, or trade as to justify an expectation that it will be observed with respect to a particular agreement. It may include a system of rules regularly observed even though particular rules are changed from time to time.

（2）The existence and scope of a usage of trade are to be determined as questions of fact. If a usage is embodied in a written trade code or similar writing the interpretation of the writing is to be determined by the court as a question of law.

（3）Unless otherwise agreed, a usage of trade in the vocation or trade in which the parties are engaged or a usage of trade of which they know or have reason to know gives meaning to or supplements or qualifies their agreement.

第 222 条　行业惯例

（1）行业惯例，是指某个地方、职业或者行业惯常性地遵守，因而可以合理地期待某个具体协议也会遵守的惯例。行业惯例可以包含被惯常遵守的规则体系，尽管具体规则会不时发生改变。

（2）行业惯例的存在与否及存在范围作为事实问题进行确定。行业惯例体现为书面的行业规范或者类似书面文件的，书面文件的解释由法院作为法律问题进行确定。

（3）除另有约定以外，当事人都从事的职业或者行业存在的行业惯例，或者都知道或者有理由知道的行业惯例，对协议赋予意义，或者补充、限制协议。

§ 223. Course of Dealing

（1）A course of dealing is a sequence of previous conduct between the parties to an agreement which is fairly to be regarded as establishing a common basis of understanding for interpreting their expressions and other conduct.

（2）Unless otherwise agreed, a course of dealing between the parties gives meaning to or supplements or qualifies their agreements.

第 223 条　交易历史

（1）交易历史，是指可以公平地视为确立了解释协议当事人的表述和其他行为的共同理解基础的、当事人之间的系列先前行为。

（2）除另有约定以外，当事人之间的交易历史对协议赋予意义，或者补充、限制协议。

TOPIC 5. CONDITIONS AND SIMILAR EVENTS
第五节　条件和类似事件

§ 224. Condition Defined

A condition is an event, not certain to occur, which must occur, unless its non-occurrence is excused, before performance under a contract becomes due.

第 224 条　条件的定义

条件，是指不确定会发生但（除被免责以外）必须发生，然后合同义务才应予履行的事件。

§ 225. Effects of the Non-Occurrence of a Condition

(1) Performance of a duty subject to a condition cannot become due unless the condition occurs or its non-occurrence is excused.

(2) Unless it has been excused, the non-occurrence of a condition discharges the duty when the condition can no longer occur.

(3) Non-occurrence of a condition is not a breach by a party unless he is under a duty that the condition occur.

第 225 条　条件不成就的效力

(1) 义务的履行取决于条件的，只有在条件成就或者不成就被免责时才应予履行。

(2) 除条件的不成就被免责以外，条件不可能再成就的，履行义务解除。

(3) 条件的不成就不是当事人违约，但其承担了条件成就义务的除外。

§ 226. How an Event May Be Made a Condition

An event may be made a condition either by the agreement of the parties or by a term supplied by the court.

第 226 条　事件如何成为条件

经当事人协议一致或者经法院补充条款，事件可以成为条件。

§ 227. Standards of Preference with Regard to Conditions

（1）In resolving doubts as to whether an event is made a condition of an obligor's duty, and as to the nature of such an event, an interpretation is preferred that will reduce the obligee's risk of forfeiture, unless the event is within the obligee's control or the circumstances indicate that he has assumed the risk.

（2）Unless the contract is of a type under which only one party generally undertakes duties, when it is doubtful whether

（a）a duty is imposed on an obligee that an event occur, or

（b）the event is made a condition of the obligor's duty, or

（c）the event is made a condition of the obligor's duty and a duty is imposed on the obligee that the event occur,

the first interpretation is preferred if the event is within the obligee's control.

（3）In case of doubt, an interpretation under which an event is a condition of an obligor's duty is preferred over an interpretation under which the non-occurrence of the event is a ground for discharge of that duty after it has become a duty to perform.

第 227 条　条件的优先标准

（1）对某事件是否是义务人义务的条件以及事件性质存在疑问的，优先采用降低权利人没收风险的解释，但若事件处于权利人控制之中，或者有证据表明权利人承担了这一风险的除外。

（2）除合同属于通常只有一方当事人承担义务的情形以外，存在下列疑问时：

（a）向权利人施加了事件发生的义务，还是

（b）将事件约定为义务人义务的条件，还是

（c）将事件约定为义务人义务的条件，且向权利人施加了事件发生的

义务，

事件处于权利人控制之中的，第一种解释优先。

（3）存在疑问时，优先解释为事件是义务人义务的条件，而非解释为履行义务产生后事件的不发生是解除义务的理由。

§ 228. Satisfaction of the Obligor as a Condition

When it is a condition of an obligor's duty that he be satisfied with respect to the obligee's performance or with respect to something else, and it is practicable to determine whether a reasonable person in the position of the obligor would be satisfied, an interpretation is preferred under which the condition occurs if such a reasonable person in the position of the obligor would be satisfied.

第 228 条　义务人的满意作为条件

义务人义务的条件是对权利人的履行或者对其他事情感到满意，且确定处于义务人地位的理性常人是否满意是可行的，处于义务人地位的理性常人满意则条件成就的解释优先。

§ 229. Excuse of a Condition to Avoid Forfeiture

To the extent that the non-occurrence of a condition would cause disproportionate forfeiture, a court may excuse the non-occurrence of that condition unless its occurrence was a material part of the agreed exchange.

第 229 条　为避免没收而对条件免责

条件的不成就会导致不成比例的没收的，在此范围内法院可以对条件的不成就免责，但条件的成就是约定交换的重要部分的除外。

§ 230. Event That Terminates a Duty

（1）Except as stated in Subsection（2），if under the terms of the contract the occurrence of an event is to terminate an obligor's duty of immediate performance or one to pay damages for breach, that duty is discharged if the event occurs.

（2）The obligor's duty is not discharged if occurrence of the event

（a）is the result of a breach by the obligor of his duty of good faith and fair dealing, or

（b）could not have been prevented because of impracticability and continuance of the duty does not subject the obligor to a materially increased burden.

（3）The obligor's duty is not discharged if, before the event occurs, the obligor promises to perform the duty even if the event occurs and does not revoke his promise before the obligee materially changes his position in reliance on it.

第 230 条 终止义务的事件

（1）除第（2）款所述规则以外，合同条款规定，事件的发生将终止义务人立即履行义务或者支付违约损害赔偿金义务的，事件发生时义务解除。

（2）事件的发生有下列情形的，义务人的义务不解除：

（a）是义务人违反自己的善意与公平交易义务的结果的，或者

（b）由于履行不能而无法避免，且义务的持续并不给义务人显著增加负担的。

（3）义务人在事件发生之前允诺，即使事件发生也会履行义务，且在权利人因产生信赖而实质性改变地位之前没有撤销允诺的，义务人的义务不解除。

第十章

履行与不履行

Chapter 10

PERFORMANCE AND
NON-PERFORMANCE

TOPIC 1. PERFORMANCES TO BE EXCHANGED UNDER AN EXCHANGE OF PROMISES
第一节　允诺交换项下的履行交换

§ 231. Criterion for Determining When Performances Are to Be Exchanged Under an Exchange of Promises

Performances are to be exchanged under an exchange of promises if each promise is at least part of the consideration for the other and the performance of each promise is to be exchanged at least in part for the performance of the other.

第 231 条　判断何时进行允诺交换项下的履行交换的标准

每个允诺至少是向对方允诺提供的部分对价，且每个允诺的履行至少部分地为了换取对方允诺的履行的，需要进行允诺交换规定的履行交换。

§ 232. When It Is Presumed That Performances Are to Be Exchanged Under an Exchange of Promises

Where the consideration given by each party to a contract consists in whole or in part of promises, all the performances to be rendered by each party taken collectively are treated as performances to be exchanged under an exchange of promises, unless a contrary intention is clearly manifested.

第 232 条　何时推定需要进行允诺交换项下的履行交换

合同各方当事人给予的对价全部或者部分是允诺的，各方当事人所有待给付履行总体视为允诺交换项下需要进行的履行交换，但存在清晰的相反意思表示的除外。

§ 233. Performance at One Time or in Installments

(1) Where performances are to be exchanged under an exchange of promises, and the whole of one party's performance can be rendered at one time, it is due at one time, unless the language or the circumstances indicate the contrary.

(2) Where only a part of one party's performance is due at one time under Subsection (1), if the other party's performance can be so apportioned that there is a comparable part that can also be rendered at that time, it is due at that time, unless the language or the circumstances indicate the contrary.

第 233 条 一次性履行还是分期履行

(1) 根据允诺交换进行履行交换，且一方当事人的全部履行可以一次性给付的，全部履行一次性到期，但语言或者情形具有相反表示的除外。

(2) 一方当事人只有部分履行是第（1）款规定的一次性到期的，如果对方的履行也能划分为具有可比性的能够在同一时间给付的部分履行的，部分履行在这一时间到期，但语言或者情形有相反表示的除外。

§ 234. Order of Performances

(1) Where all or part of the performances to be exchanged under an exchange of promises can be rendered simultaneously, they are to that extent due simultaneously, unless the language or the circumstances indicate the contrary.

(2) Except to the extent stated in Subsection (1), where the performance of only one party under such an exchange requires a period of time, his performance is due at an earlier time than that of the other party, unless the language or the circumstances indicate the contrary.

第 234 条 履行顺序

(1) 根据允诺交换进行交换的履行，全部或者部分可以同时给付的，在此范围内同时到期，但语言或者情形有相反表示的除外。

(2) 除第（1）款所述规则以外，这种交换中只有一方当事人的履行需要一段时间的，该当事人的履行在早于对方的时间到期，但语言或者情形有相反表示的除外。

TOPIC 2. EFFECT OF PERFORMANCE AND NON−PERFORMANCE
第二节　履行和不履行的效力

§ 235. Effect of Performance as Discharge and of Non−Performance as Breach

（1）Full performance of a duty under a contract discharges the duty.

（2）When performance of a duty under a contract is due any non−performance is a breach.

第 235 条　履行产生义务解除、不履行构成违约的效力

（1）对合同义务的完全履行解除合同义务。

（2）合同规定的义务到期时，任何不履行都是违约。

§ 236. Claims for Damages for Total and For Partial Breach

（1）A claim for damages for total breach is one for damages based on all of the injured party's remaining rights to performance.

（2）A claim for damages for partial breach is one for damages based on only part of the injured party's remaining rights to performance.

第 236 条　完全违约和部分违约的损害赔偿请求权

（1）完全违约的损害赔偿请求权，是基于受害人对履行的所有剩余权利的损害赔偿请求权。

（2）部分违约的损害赔偿请求权，是基于受害人对履行的部分剩余权利的损害赔偿请求权。

§ 237. Effect on Other Party's Duties of a Failure to Render Performance

Except as stated in §240, it is a condition of each party's remaining duties to render performances to be exchanged under an exchange of promises that there be no uncured material failure by the other party to render any such performance due at an earlier time.

第 237 条 没能给付履行对他方当事人义务的效力

除第 240 条所述规则以外，各方当事人有义务给付允诺交换项下的待交换履行的条件，是对方先到期的此类履行没有任何未予补救的重大不给付情况。

§ 238. Effect on Other Party's Duties of a Failure to Offer Performance

Where all or part of the performances to be exchanged under an exchange of promises are due simultaneously, it is a condition of each party's duties to render such performance that the other party either render or, with manifested present ability to do so, offer performance of his part of the simultaneous exchange.

第 238 条 没有提出履行对他方当事人义务的效力

允诺交换项下的履行交换全部或者部分同时到期的，各方当事人给付履行义务的条件，是对方当事人给付同时交换中的己方履行，或者明显具有立即履行的能力并提出履行。

§ 239. Effect on Other Party's Duties of a Failure Justified by Non-Occurrence of a Condition

(1) A party's failure to render or to offer performance may, except as stated in Subsection (2), affect the other party's duties under the rules stated in §§ 237 and 238 even though failure is justified by the non-occurrence of a condition.

(2) The rule stated in Subsection (1) does not apply if the other party assumed the risk that he would have to perform in spite of such a failure.

第 239 条　条件未成就使得未能履行成为合理时对他方义务的效力

（1）当事人未给付履行或者未提出履行的，除第（2）款所述规则以外，可能会影响第 237 条、第 238 条所述规则规定的对方当事人的义务，即使因条件未成就未能履行是合理的。

（2）对方当事人承担了即使存在上述未能履行自己也必须履行的风险的，第（1）款所述规则不予适用。

§ 240. Part Performances as Agreed Equivalents

If the performances to be exchanged under an exchange of promises can be apportioned into corresponding pairs of part performances so that the parts of each pair are properly regarded as agreed equivalents, a party's performance of his part of such a pair has the same effect on the other's duties to render performance of the agreed equivalent as it would have if only that pair of performances had been promised.

第 240 条　部分履行作为约定的对等履行

如果允诺交换项下的待交换履行可以划分为相应的部分履行的组合，因而每个组合中的对应部分可以适宜地看作是约定的对等履行的，当事人履行了组合中的己方部分对于对方给付约定的对等履行义务的效力，与当事人只允诺了该履行组合的效果相同。

§ 241. Circumstances Significant in Determining Whether a Failure Is Material

In determining whether a failure to render or to offer performance is material, the following circumstances are significant:

（a）the extent to which the injured party will be deprived of the benefit which he reasonably expected;

（b）the extent to which the injured party can be adequately compensated for the part of that benefit of which he will be deprived;

（c）the extent to which the party failing to perform or to offer to perform will suffer forfeiture;

（d）the likelihood that the party failing to perform or to offer to perform will cure his failure, taking account of all the circumstances including any reasonable assurances;

（e）the extent to which the behavior of the party failing to perform or to offer to perform comports with standards of good faith and fair dealing.

第 241 条　确定未能履行是否重大时的重要情形

确定未能给付履行或者提出履行是否重大时，下列情形具有重要意义：

（a）受害人在何种程度上会被剥夺合理期待的利益；

（b）受害人在何种程度上能够得到被剥夺利益的充分补偿；

（c）没有履行或者提出履行的当事人在多大程度上将会遭到没收；

（d）虑及包括合理保证[1]在内的所有情形，没有履行或者提出履行的当事人补救自己行为的可能性大小；

（e）没有履行或者提出履行的当事人，其行为在多大程度上符合善意与公平交易标准。

§ 242. Circumstances Significant in Determining When Remaining Duties are Discharged

In determining the time after which a party's uncured material failure to render or to offer performance discharges the other party's remaining duties to render performance under the rules stated in §§ 237 and 238, the following circumstances are significant:

（a）those stated in § 241;

（b）the extent to which it reasonably appears to the injured party that delay may prevent or hinder him in making reasonable substitute arrangements;

（c）the extent to which the agreement provides for performance without delay, but a material failure to perform or to offer to perform on a stated day does not of itself discharge the other party's remaining duties unless the circumstances, including the language of the agreement, indicate that performance or an offer to perform by

---

〔1〕　合理保证（reasonable assurance），参见第 251 条的注释。

that day is important.

第 242 条　确定尚未履行义务何时解除的重要情形

当事人未能给付履行或者提出履行，这一重大违约行为在特定时间之后未经补救的，第 237 条和第 238 条规定的对方当事人尚未履行的合同义务得以解除；在确定这一时间时，下列情形具有重要意义：

（a）第 241 条所述情形；

（b）受害人在多大程度上可以合理地认为，迟延可能阻却或者阻碍自己作出合理的替代安排；

（c）协议在何种程度上规定毫不迟延地履行，但是，除包括协议语言在内的情形表明，在当日之前履行或者提出履行是至关重要的以外，未在所述日期履行或者提出履行这一重大违约并不自然地解除对方当事人尚未履行的义务。

§ 243. Effect of a Breach by Non-Performance as Giving Rise to a Claim for Damages for Total Breach

（1）With respect to performances to be exchanged under an exchange of promises, a breach by non-performance gives rise to a claim for damages for total breach only if it discharges the injured party's remaining duties to render such performance, other than a duty to render an agreed equivalent under § 240.

（2）Except as stated in Subsection （3）, a breach by non-performance accompanied or followed by a repudiation gives rise to a claim for damage for total breach.

（3）Where at the time of the breach the only remaining duties of performance are those of the party in breach and are for the payment of money in installments not related to one another, his breach by non-performance as to less than the whole, whether or not accompanied or followed by a repudiation, does not give rise to a claim for damages for total breach.

（4）In any case other than those stated in the preceding subsections, a breach by non-performance gives rise to a claim for total breach only if it so substantially impairs the value of the contract to the injured party at the time of the breach that it is just in the circumstances to allow him to recover damages based on all his remaining rights to performance.

第 243 条　不履行违约产生违约损害赔偿请求权的效力

（1）对于允诺交换项下的待交换履行，不履行产生的违约[1]只有在导致受害人尚未履行的合同义务解除时，而非第 240 条规定的给付约定的对等履行义务解除时，才产生完全违约损害赔偿请求权。

（2）除第（3）款所述规则以外，不履行违约伴随或者随后发生拒绝履行的，产生完全违约损害赔偿请求权。

（3）违约产生之时，唯一剩余的履行义务是违约方的义务，而且是分期支付各期互不相关的金钱义务的，违约方针对少于整体的不履行违约，无论是否伴随着或者随后发生了拒绝履行，都不产生完全违约损害赔偿请求权。

（4）除上述几款所述情形以外，只有在违约产生时实质性地损害了受害人的合同价值，因而允许其基于对履行的所有剩余权利取得损害赔偿在具体情形下是公平的，不履行违约方才产生完全违约损害赔偿请求权。

§ 244. Effect of Subsequent Events on Duty to Pay Damages

A party's duty to pay damages for total breach by non-performance is discharged if it appears after the breach that there would have been a total failure by the injured party to perform his return promise.

第 244 条　随后发生的事件对支付损害赔偿金义务的效力

当事人因不履行而产生完全违约之后，表面情况表明受害人本来就完全不能履行其回报允诺的，损害赔偿金的支付义务解除。

§ 245. Effect of a Breach by Non-Performance As Excusing the Non-Occurrence of a Condition

Where a party's breach by non-performance contributes materially to the non-occurrence of a condition of one of his duties, the non-occurrence is excused.

---

[1]　不履行产生的违约（a breach by non-performance），为避免表述过于复杂，下文统一简称为"不履行违约"。

第245条　不履行违约构成条件不成就免责的效力

当事人的不履行违约实质性地促成了其义务之一的条件不成就的，不成就免责。

§ 246. Effect of Acceptance as Excusing the Non-Occurrence of a Condition

(1) Except as stated in Subsection (2), an obligor's acceptance or his retention for an unreasonable time of the obligee's performance, with knowledge of or reason to know of the non-occurrence of a condition of the obligor's duty, operates as a promise to perform in spite of that non-occurrence, under the rules stated in § 84.

(2) If at the time of its acceptance or retention the obligee's performance involves such attachment to the obligor's property that removal would cause material loss, the obligor's acceptance or retention of that performance operates as a promise to perform in spite of the non-occurrence of the condition, under the rules stated in § 84, only if the obligor with knowledge of or reason to know of the defects manifests assent to the performance.

第246条　接受构成对条件不成就免责的效力

（1）除第（2）款所述规则以外，义务人知道或者有理由知道义务人履行义务的条件并未成就，但仍然接受了或者在一段不合理的时间内保留了权利人的履行的，即为作出第84条所述规则规定的条件不成就也会履行的允诺。

（2）如果义务人接受或者保留履行之时，权利人的履行涉及义务人财产的附属物且移除会导致重大损失，则只有知道或者有理由知道该瑕疵的义务人对履行作出同意表示的，他对履行的接受或者保留才是第84条所述规则规定的即使条件不出现也会履行的允诺。

§ 247. Effect of Acceptance of Part Performance as Excusing the Subsequent Non-Occurrence of a Condition

An obligor's acceptance of part of the obligee's performance, with knowledge or reason to know of the non-occurrence of a condition of the obligor's duty, operates as a promise to perform in spite of a subsequent non-occurrence of the condition under the rules stated in §84 to the extent that it justifies the obligee in believing that subsequent performances will be accepted in spite of that non-occurrence.

第 247 条　接受部分履行构成对随后条件不成就免责的效力

义务人知道或者有理由知道其履行义务的条件并未成就，但接受了权利人的部分履行的，在权利人合理地认为即使条件不成就随后的履行也会被接受的范围之内，义务人即为作出了第84条所述规则规定的即使随后条件不成就也会履行的允诺。

§ 248. Effect of Insufficient Reason for Rejection as Excusing the Non-Occurrence of a Condition

Where a party rejecting a defective performance or offer of performance gives an insufficient reason for rejection, the non-occurrence of a condition of his duty is excused only if he knew or had reason to know of that non-occurrence and then only to the extent that the giving of an insufficient reason substantially contributes to a failure by the other party to cure.

第 248 条　不充分的拒绝理由构成对条件不成就免责的效力

拒绝接受瑕疵履行或者提出的履行的当事人给出了不充分的拒绝理由的，只有在他本来就知道或者有理由知道自己承担义务的条件不成就，然后给出的不充分理由实质性地促成了对方当事人未能进行补救的，方可构成免责义务条件的不成就。

§ 249. When Payment Other Than by Legal Tender Is Sufficient

Where the payment or offer of payment of money is made a condition of an obligor's duty, payment or offer of payment in any manner current in the ordinary course of business satisfies the requirement unless the obligee demands payment in legal tender and gives any extension of time reasonably necessary to procure it.

第 249 条　何时使用非法定货币[1]支付是充分[2]的

支付金钱或者提出支付是义务人的义务条件的，按照当前一般商业过程中通常使用的任何方式支付或者提出支付都满足这一要求，但权利人要求使用法定货币支付并提供了获取法定货币所必须的合理期限的除外。

TOPIC 3. EFFECT OF PROSPECTIVE NON-PERFORMANCE
第三节　预期不履行的效力

§ 250. When a Statement or an Act Is a Repudiation

A repudiation is

(a) a statement by the obligor to the obligee indicating that the obligor will commit a breach that would of itself give the obligee a claim for damages for total breach under § 243, or

(b) a voluntary affirmative act which renders the obligor unable or apparently unable to perform without such a breach.

---

〔1〕　法定货币（legal tender），本条中的"tender"是"金钱"（money）的意思。请对照第 45 条注释，并参阅 Garner（2009：1606）以及"重述"原文的本条评论。

〔2〕　此处"充分"对应原文"sufficient"。本书中译作"充分"的原文有两个：sufficient 与 adequate（不区分词性）。根据有关文献和译者个人体会，虽然两词有时候可以互换使用，但是前者使用的语境总是暗示一定的规则、标准、原则等，而后者似乎更强调程度。例如 sufficient consideration 强调对价的合法性，而 adequate consideration 则强调对价的公平性。再如，本条的 sufficient 表示使用法定货币符合规则要求；第 251 条中的 adequate assurance 指足以达到让权利人能够确信义务人将适当履行的程度，如此等等。请读者对照相关中英表述进行查验、指正，不再另行说明。

第 250 条　何时陈述或者行为构成拒绝履行

拒绝履行是指：

（a）义务人向权利人作出的陈述，说明义务人将要违约，并且违约会自然使权利人产生第 243 条规定的完全违约损害赔偿请求权，或者

（b）没有上述违约时，使得义务人不能或者明显不能履行的主动、明确的行为。

§ 251. When a Failure to Give Assurance May Be Treated As a Repudiation

（1）Where reasonable grounds arise to believe that the obligor will commit a breach by non-performance that would of itself give the obligee a claim for damages for total breach under § 243, the obligee may demand adequate assurance of due performance and may, if reasonable, suspend any performance for which he has not already received the agreed exchange until he receives such assurance.

（2）The obligee may treat as a repudiation the obligor's failure to provide within a reasonable time such assurance of due performance as is adequate in the circumstances of the particular case.

第 251 条　何时未能提供保证可以视为拒绝履行

（1）有合理理由相信义务人将会产生不履行违约，且违约会自然赋予权利人第 243 条规定的完全违约损害赔偿请求权的，权利人可以要求提供适当履行所需的充分保证〔1〕，如果合理，也可以中止尚未收到的约定交换对应的

---

〔1〕　充分保证（adequate assurance），根据译者个人理解，assurance 一词虽然译为"保证"，但此处含义和我国《担保法》中的"保证"和"担保"都不相同，其核心意义是"给别人带来信心"、"让人确信"，与其动词形式"assure"的通用含义相似。高凌云教授认为，assurance 在实务中有时称作"安慰函"，但本书中的处理也可以接受。根据 Garner（2009）的解释，在合同法语境中，"adequate assurance"是指"能让合同权利人产生合理信心，认为合同会得以适当履行的情形或者合同义务人的行为"；如果权利人因为合理的原因产生不安全感（feel insecure），并公平地要求提供保证（assurance），那么义务人不提供充分保证就会构成拒绝履行合同。保证何时充分是个事实问题，有时候打电话进行口头说明或者解释也是充分的保证（见"重述"原文本条评论 e 以及相关示例）。第 252 条的"保证"意义相同。

任何履行，直至收到保证为止。

（2）义务人在合理期间内未能提供具体情况下适当履行所需的充分保证的，权利人可以视为拒绝履行。

§ 252. Effect of Insolvency

（1）Where the obligor's insolvency gives the obligee reasonable grounds to believe that the obligor will commit a breach under the rule stated in §251, the obligee may suspend any performance for which he has not already received the agreed exchange until he receives assurance in the form of performance itself, an offer of performance, or adequate security.

（2）A person is insolvent who either has ceased to pay his debts in the ordinary course of business or cannot pay his debts as they become due or is insolvent within the meaning of the federal bankruptcy law.

第 252 条 无力偿债的效力

（1）由于义务人无力偿债而使得权利人有合理理由相信，义务人将产生第 251 条所述规则规定的违约行为的，权利人可以中止尚未收到的约定交换的履行，直至收到以履行本身、提出履行或者充分担保形式提供的保证为止。

（2）在正常经营过程中停止偿还债务，债务到期时不能偿还债务，或者处于联邦破产法意义上的无力偿债状况的，是无力偿债。

§ 253. Effect of a Repudiation as a Breach and on Other Party's Duties

（1）Where an obligor repudiates a duty before he has committed a breach by non-performance and before he has received all of the agreed exchange for it, his repudiation alone gives rise to a claim for damages for total breach.

（2）Where performances are to be exchanged under an exchange of promises, one party's repudiation of a duty to render performance discharges the other's remaining duties to render performance.

第 253 条　拒绝履行作为违约的效力以及对他方当事人义务的效力

（1）义务人在不履行违约之前，并在收到己方义务对应的所有约定交换之前，拒绝履行义务的，拒绝履行本身足以产生完全违约损害赔偿请求权。

（2）根据允诺交换进行履行交换时，一方当事人拒绝履行义务的，对方当事人尚未履行的合同义务解除。

§ 254. Effect of Subsequent Events on Duty to Pay Damages

（1）A party's duty to pay damages for total breach by repudiation is discharged if it appears after the breach that there would have been a total failure by the injured party to perform his return promise.

（2）A party's duty to pay damages for total breach by repudiation is discharged if it appears after the breach that the duty that he repudiated would have been discharged by impracticability or frustration before any breach by non-performance.

第 254 条　随后事件对支付损害赔偿金义务的效力

（1）当事人因拒绝履行而完全违约之后，表面情况表明受害人本来也会完全不能履行回报允诺的，当事人支付损害赔偿金的义务解除。

（2）当事人因拒绝履行而完全违约之后，表面情况表明他所拒绝履行的义务本来也会因履行不能或者目的落空而在不履行违约之前被解除的，当事人支付损害赔偿金的义务解除。

§ 255. Effect of a Repudiation as Excusing the Non-Occurrence of a Condition

Where a party's repudiation contributes materially to the non-occurrence of a condition of one of his duties, the non-occurrence is excused.

第 255 条　拒绝履行构成对条件不成就免责的效力

当事人拒绝履行实质性地促成了其义务之一的条件不成就的，该条件的不成就免责。

§ 256. Nullification of Repudiation or Basis for Repudiation

（1）The effect of a statement as constituting a repudiation under §250 or the basis for a repudiation under §251 is nullified by a retraction of the statement if notification of the retraction comes to the attention of the injured party before he materially changes his position in reliance on the repudiation or indicates to the other party that he considers the repudiation to be final.

（2）The effect of events other than a statement as constituting a repudiation under §250 or the basis for a repudiation under §251 is nullified if, to the knowledge of the injured party, those events have ceased to exist before he materially changes his position in reliance on the repudiation or indicates to the other party that he considers the repudiation to be final.

第 256 条　拒绝履行或者拒绝履行的基础归于无效

（1）构成第 250 条规定的拒绝履行或者第 251 条规定的拒绝履行基础的陈述，如果在受害人因对拒绝履行产生信赖而实质性改变地位之前，或者在受害人向对方当事人表明他认为拒绝履行是最终性的之前被撤回，且撤回通知进入了受害人注意范围的，则陈述效力归于消灭。

（2）除了陈述之外，其他构成第 250 条规定的拒绝履行或者第 251 条规定的拒绝履行基础的事件，如果据受害人所知，在受害人因对拒绝履行产生信赖而实质性改变地位之前，或者在受害人向对方当事人表明他认为拒绝履行是最终性的之前已经不再存在的，则事件的效力归于消灭。

§ 257. Effect of Urging Performance in Spite of Repudiation

The injured party does not change the effect of a repudiation by urging the repudiator to perform in spite of his repudiation or to retract his repudiation.

第 257 条　存在拒绝履行仍然催告履行的效力

发生拒绝履行的，受害人催告拒绝人履行或者撤回拒绝，不改变拒绝履行的效力。

TOPIC 4. APPLICATION OF PERFORMANCES
第四节 履行的分配

§ 258. Obligor's Direction of Application

（1）Except as stated in Subsection（2）, as between two or more contractual duties owed by an obligor to the same obligee, a performance is applied according to a direction made by the obligor to the obligee at or before the time of performance.

（2）If the obligor is under a duty to a third person to devote a performance to the discharge of a particular duty that the obligor owes to the obligee and the obligee knows or has reason to know this, the obligor's performance is applied to that duty.

第 258 条　义务人的分配指示

（1）除第（2）款所述规则以外，义务人对同一权利人负有两个或者两个以上合同义务的，根据义务人在履行时或者履行前对权利人的指示进行履行分配。

（2）义务人对第三人负有义务，应当将履行用于解除义务人对权利人负有的特定义务，且权利人知道或者有理由知道的，义务人的履行适用于该特定义务。

§ 259. Creditor's Application

（1）Except as stated in Subsections（2）and（3）, if the debtor has not directed application of a payment as between two or more matured debts, the payment is applied according to a manifestation of intention made within a reasonable time by the creditor to the debtor.

（2）A creditor cannot apply such a payment to a debt if

（a）the debtor could not have directed its application to that debt, or

（b）a forfeiture would result from a failure to apply it to another debt and the creditor knows or has reason to know this, or

（c）the debt is disputed or is unenforceable on grounds of public policy.

（3）If a creditor is owed one such debt in his own right and another in a fiduciary capacity, he cannot, unless empowered to do so by the beneficiary, effectively apply to the debt in his own right a greater proportion of a payment than that borne by the unsecured portion of that debt to the unsecured portions of both claims.

第 259 条　债权人的分配

（1）除第（2）款和第（3）款所述规则以外，债务人没有在两个或者两个以上到期债务之间作出偿付分配指示的，根据合理期限内债权人向债务人作出的意思表示分配偿付。

（2）债权人不得将偿付分配于有下列情形的债务：

（a）债务人不可能指示将偿付分配于该债务的，或者

（b）不将偿付分配于另一债务会产生没收，且债权人知道或者有理由知道的，或者

（c）债务有争议，或者基于公共政策是不可强制执行的。

（3）债权人自身对一项债务拥有权利，又以受托人的身份对另一项债务拥有权利，除经受益人授权以外，不能有效地使得自己债务的偿付分配比例超过自己债务未经担保部分在两个债务未经担保部分的总和中所占的比例[1]。

§ 260. Application of Payments Where Neither Party Exercises His Power

（1）If neither the debtor nor the creditor has exercised his power with respect to the application of a payment as between two or more matured debts, the payment is applied to debts to which the creditor could have applied it with just regard to the interests of third persons, the debtor and the creditor.

（2）In applying payments under the rule stated in Subsection（1）, a payment is applied to the earliest matured debt and ratably among debts of the same maturity, except that preference is given

（a）to a debt that the debtor is under a duty to a third person to pay immediately, and

---

〔1〕　该表示比较拗口，简而言之就是，自己债务的偿付比例≤自己债务未经担保部分/两个债务未经担保部分之和（斜杠左侧表示分子，右侧表示分母）。

（b）if he is not under such a duty,

    （i）to overdue interest rather than principal, and

    （ii）to an unsecured or precarious debt rather than one that is secured or

        certain of payment.

第 260 条　当事人都不行使权利时的偿付分配

（1）债务人和债权人都没有行使两项或者两项以上到期债务之间的偿付分配权的，根据债权人若公平考虑第三人、债务人和债权人的利益后将会适用的债务进行分配。

（2）根据第（1）款所述规则进行偿付分配时，首先偿付最先到期的债务，按比例分配于同时到期的债务，但应优先偿付：

（a）债务人对第三人负有立即偿付义务的债务，和

（b）债务人没有上述义务时，

    （i）逾期利息而非本金，和

    （ii）未经担保或是缺乏保障的债务，而非有担保或者确定能偿付的

        债务。

第十一章

履行不能与目的落空

Chapter 11
IMPRACTICABILITY OF
PERFORMANCE AND
FRUSTRATION OF PURPOSE

§ 261. Discharge by Supervening Impracticability

Where, after a contract is made, a party's performance is made impracticable without his fault by the occurrence of an event the non-occurrence of which was a basic assumption on which the contract was made, his duty to render that performance is discharged, unless the language or the circumstances indicate the contrary.

第 261 条　因继起的履行不能而解除

合同订立之后，当事人没有过错而因某一事件的发生导致其履行不现实，且事件的不发生是合同订立的基本假设的，其履行该合同的义务解除，但语言和情形具有相反意思表示的除外。

§ 262. Death or Incapacity of Person Necessary for Performance

If the existence of a particular person is necessary for the performance of a duty, his death or such incapacity as makes performance impracticable is an event the non-occurrence of which was a basic assumption on which the contract was made.

第 262 条　履行所必需的人死亡或者丧失行为能力

特定人的存在是履行义务所必需的，该人的死亡或者导致履行不能的行为能力缺失，是合同订立时被认为不会发生的基本假设事件。

§ 263. Destruction, Deterioration or Failure to Come into Existence of Thing Necessary for Performance

If the existence of a specific thing is necessary for the performance of a duty, its failure to come into existence, destruction, or such deterioration as makes performance impracticable is an event the non-occurrence of which was a basic assumption on which the contract was made.

第 263 条　履行义务所必需的事物的毁损、腐坏或者未能产生

如果特定事物的存在是义务履行所必需的，该事物未能产生、被毁损或者出现导致履行不能的腐坏，是合同订立时被认为不会发生的基本假设事件。

§ 264. Prevention by Governmental Regulation or Order

If the performance of a duty is made impracticable by having to comply with a domestic or foreign governmental regulation or order, that regulation or order is an event the non-occurrence of which was a basic assumption on which the contract was made.

第 264 条　因政府规章或者法令而受阻却

由于必须遵守国内或者国外的政府规章或者命令使得义务履行成为不现实的，该规章或者命令是合同订立时被认为不会发生的基本假设事件。

§ 265. Discharge by Supervening Frustration

Where, after a contract is made, a party's principal purpose is substantially frustrated without his fault by the occurrence of an event the non-occurrence of which was a basic assumption on which the contract was made, his remaining duties to render performance are discharged, unless the language or the circumstances indicate the contrary.

第 265 条　因继起的目的落空而解除

合同订立之后，当事人没有过错而因某一事件的发生导致其主要目的实质上落空，且事件的不发生是合同订立的基本假设的，其未履行的合同义务解除，但语言或者情形有相反表示的除外。

§ 266. Existing Impracticability or Frustration

(1) Where, at the time a contract is made, a party's performance under it is impracticable without his fault because of a fact of which he has no reason to know

and the non-existence of which is a basic assumption on which the contract is made, no duty to render that performance arises, unless the language or circumstances indicate the contrary.

(2) Where, at the time a contract is made, a party's principal purpose is substantially frustrated without his fault by a fact of which he has no reason to know and the non-existence of which is a basic assumption on which the contract is made, no duty of that party to render performance arises, unless the language or circumstances indicate the contrary.

第 266 条　现有的履行不能或者目的落空

(1) 合同订立之时，由于当事人没有理由知道的事实而使得其履行不现实且当事人没有过错，该事实的不存在也是合同订立的基本假设的，不产生给付该履行的义务，但语言或者情形有相反表示的除外。

(2) 合同订立之时，由于当事人没有理由知道的事实而使得其主要目的实质性落空且当事人没有过错，该事实的不存在也是合同订立的基本假设的，不产生该当事人给付履行的义务，但语言或者情形有相反表示的除外。

§ 267. Effect on Other Party's Duties of a Failure Justified by Impracticability or Frustration

(1) A party's failure to render or to offer performance may, except as stated in Subsection (2), affect the other party's duties under the rules stated in §§ 237 and 238 even though the failure is justified under the rules stated in this Chapter.

(2) The rule stated in Subsection (1) does not apply if the other party assumed the risk that he would have to perform despite such a failure.

第 267 条　因履行不能或者目的落空使得不履行合理化对他方当事人义务的效力

(1) 除第 (2) 款所述规定以外，当事人未能给付履行或者提出履行的，即使根据本章所述规则是合理的，根据第 237 条和第 238 条所述规则也可能影响对方当事人的义务。

（2）对方当事人承担了即使对方未能给付履行或者提出履行自己也必须履行的风险的，第（1）款所述规则不适用。

§ 268. Effect on Other Party's Duties of a Prospective Failure Justified by Impracticability or Frustration

（1）A party's prospective failure of performance may, except as stated in Subsection (2), discharge the other party's duties or allow him to suspend performance under the rules stated in §§ 251 (1) and 253 (2) even though the failure would be justified under the rules stated in this Chapter.

（2）The rule stated in Subsection (1) does not apply if the other party assumed the risk that he would have to perform in spite of such a failure.

第 268 条　因履行不能或者目的落空使得预期不履行合理化对他方当事人义务的效力

（1）除第（2）款所述规则以外，即使当事人的预期不履行根据本章所述规则是合理的，也可以根据第 251（1）条和第 253（2）条所述规则解除对方当事人义务，或者允许对方当事人中止履行。

（2）对方当事人承担了即使对方预期不履行自己也必须履行的风险的，第（1）款所述规则不予适用。

§ 269. Temporary Impracticability or Frustration

Impracticability of performance or frustration of purpose that is only temporary suspends the obligor's duty to perform while the impracticability or frustration exists but does not discharge his duty or prevent it from arising unless his performance after the cessation of the impracticability or frustration would be materially more burdensome than had there been no impracticability or frustration.

第 269 条　暂时性履行不能或者目的落空

履行不能或者目的落空仅是暂时性的，义务人的履行义务在履行不能或者目的落空存在时得以中止，并不解除义务人的义务或者阻却其义务的产生；不能履行或者目的落空的情况结束之后，义务人的履行较之不发生履行不能或者目的落空时将会实质性地增加负担的除外。

§ 270. Partial Impracticability

Where only part of an obligor's performance is impracticable, his duty to render the remaining part is unaffected if

(a) it is still practicable for him to render performance that is substantial, taking account of any reasonable substitute performance that he is under a duty to render; or

(b) the obligee, within a reasonable time, agrees to render any remaining performance in full and to allow the obligor to retain any performance that has already been rendered.

第 270 条　部分履行不能

义务人的履行只是部分不能的，尚未履行的义务在下列情形下不受影响：

（a）考虑到义务人应予给付的任何合理替代履行，给付实质性履行仍然是可行的；或者

（b）权利人在合理的时间内同意完全给付任何剩余履行，并且允许义务人保留权利人已经给付的任何履行的。

§ 271. Impracticability as Excuse for Non-Occurrence of a Condition

Impracticability excuses the non-occurrence of a condition if the occurrence of the condition is not a material part of the agreed exchange and forfeiture would otherwise result.

第 271 条　履行不能构成对条件不成就免责

条件的成就不是约定的交换中的重要部分，并且不免责条件的不成就将会导致没收的，履行不能构成对条件不成就的免责。

§ 272. Relief Including Restitution

（1）In any case governed by the rules stated in this Chapter, either party may have a claim for relief including restitution under the rules stated in §§ 240 and 377.

（2）In any case governed by the rules stated in this Chapter, if those rules together with the rules stated in Chapter 16 will not avoid injustice, the court may grant relief on such terms as justice requires including protection of the parties' reliance interests.

第 272 条　包括返还的救济

（1）在受本章所述规则调整的任何情况下，任一当事人都有权依据第 240 条和第 377 条的规定请求包括返还在内的救济。

（2）在受本章所述规则调整的任何情况下，如果本章规则以及第 16 章所述规则不能避免不公正的发生，法院可以根据公正的需要给予包括保护当事人信赖利益在内的救济。

第十二章

通过同意或者
修改解除义务

Chapter 12

DISCHARGE BY ASSENT OR
ALTERATION

TOPIC 1. THE REQUIREMENT OF CONSIDERATION
第一节　对价要求

§ 273. Requirement of Consideration or a Substitute

Except as stated in §§ 274 – 77, an obligee's manifestation of assent to discharge is not effective unless

(a) it is made for consideration,

(b) it is made in circumstances in which a promise would be enforceable without consideration, or

(c) it has induced such action or forbearance as would make a promise enforceable.

第273条　对价或者对价替代的要求

除了第274~277条所述规则以外，权利人解除义务的同意表示只有在下列情形下有效：

(a) 为了取得对价而作出的，

(b) 在当时的情形下，没有对价的允诺也是可以强制执行的，或者

(c) 诱使允诺可以被强制执行的行为或者不行为发生的。

§ 274. Cancellation, Destruction or Surrender of a Writing

An obligee's cancellation, destruction or surrender to the obligor of a writing of a type customarily accepted as a symbol or as evidence of his right discharges without consideration the obligor's duty if it is done with the manifested intention to discharge it.

第274条　撤销、毁损或者交还书面文件

权利人撤销、毁损或者向义务人交还通常被认为属于其权利的标志或者证明的书面文件的，如果具有解除义务人义务的意思表示，义务人的义务也

得以解除。

§ 275. Assent to Discharge Duty of Return Performance

If a party, before he has fully performed his duty under a contract, manifests to the other party his assent to discharge the other party's duty to render part or all of the agreed exchange, the duty is to that extent discharged without consideration.

第275条　同意解除回报履行义务

在尚未完全履行合同规定的己方义务之前，当事人向对方作出表示，同意全部或者部分解除对方给付约定交换的义务的，该义务没有对价也在此范围内解除。

§ 276. Assent to Discharge Duty to Transfer Property

A duty of an obligor in possession of identified personal property to transfer an interest in that property is discharged without consideration if the obligee manifests to the obligor his assent to the discharge of that duty.

第276条　同意解除转让财产的义务

权利人向占有已特定化的动产的义务人作出表示，同意解除其转让该动产权益的义务的，该义务没有对价也得以解除。

§ 277. Renunciation

(1) A written renunciation signed and delivered by the obligee discharges without consideration a duty arising out of a breach of contract.

(2) A renunciation by the obligee on his acceptance from the obligor of some performance under a contract discharges without consideration a duty to pay damages for a breach that gives rise only to a claim for damages for partial breach of contract.

第 277 条　放弃[1]

（1）权利人在书面放弃文件上签字并交付的，违约产生的义务没有对价也得以解除。

（2）权利人接受义务人合同项下的某些履行时作出放弃的，支付违约赔偿金的义务没有对价也得以解除，但仅限于违约产生部分违约损害赔偿请求权的情况。

TOPIC 2. SUBSTITUTED PERFORMANCE, SUBSTITUTED CONTRACT, ACCORD AND ACCOUNT STATED
第二节　替代履行、替代合同，和解合同与认可账单

§ 278. Substituted Performance

（1）If an obligee accepts in satisfaction of the obligor's duty a performance offered by the obligor that differs from what is due, the duty is discharged.

（2）If an obligee accepts in satisfaction of the obligor's duty a performance offered by a third person, the duty is discharged, but an obligor who has not previously assented to the performance for his benefit may in a reasonable time after learning of it render the discharge inoperative from the beginning by disclaimer.

第 278 条　替代履行

（1）权利人接受了义务人提供的不同于到期履行的履行，以清偿义务人的义务的，义务人的义务得以解除。

（2）权利人接受了第三人提供的履行以清偿义务人的义务的，义务人的义务得以解除，但义务人此前并未对使其受益的履行表示同意的，可以在得

---

[1]　放弃（renunciation），此处也可译为"弃权"，但为了与本书的 disclaimer（"弃权"）相区别，暂作此译。renunciation 与 disclaimer 两词在"放弃权利"之意上大致相同，例如 Garner（2009）将前者释为"对权利的明确或者默示抛弃且不转让他人"，而将后者释为"对自己的法定权利或者权利请求的放弃……"；但若详加比较，两词在义项构成、语词搭配和使用语境等方面并不相同。

知此事的合理时间之内通过弃权而使得义务解除自始不产生效力。

§ 279. Substituted Contract

（1）A substituted contract is a contract that is itself accepted by the obligee in satisfaction of the obligor's existing duty.

（2）The substituted contract discharges the original duty and breach of the substituted contract by the obligor does not give the obligee a right to enforce the original duty.

第 279 条　替代合同

（1）替代合同，是指本身被权利人接受的用以清偿义务人现存义务的合同。

（2）替代合同解除原始义务；义务人违反替代合同的，并不给予权利人强制执行原始义务的权利。

§ 280. Novation

A novation is a substituted contract that includes as a party one who was neither the obligor nor the obligee of the original duty.

第 280 条　更新

更新后的合同，是指将既不是原始义务的义务人，也不是原始义务的权利人的人吸纳为当事人的替代合同。

§ 281. Accord and Satisfaction

（1）An accord is a contract under which an obligee promises to accept a stated performance in satisfaction of the obligor's existing duty. Performance of the accord discharges the original duty.

（2）Until performance of the accord, the original duty is suspended unless there is such a breach of the accord by the obligor as discharges the new duty of the obligee to accept the performance in satisfaction. If there is such a breach the obligee may enforce either the original duty or any duty under the accord.

(3) Breach of the accord by the obligee does not discharge the original duty, but the obligor may maintain a suit for specific performance of the accord, in addition to any claim for damages for partial breach.

第 281 条　和解合同与清偿

(1) 和解合同，是指权利人允诺接受所述履行以清偿义务人现有义务的合同。和解合同的履行使原始义务解除。

(2) 和解合同履行之前，原始义务中止，但义务人违反和解合同，使得权利人接受该履行作为清偿的新义务得以解除的除外。发生这种违约的，权利人可以强制执行原始合同义务，也可以强制执行和解合同规定的任何义务。

(3) 权利人违反和解合同的并不导致原始合同的义务解除，但义务人除了部分违约损害赔偿请求权以外，还可以维持具体履行和解合同的诉讼。

§ 282. Account Stated

(1) An account stated is a manifestation of assent by debtor and creditor to a stated sum as an accurate computation of an amount due the creditor. A party's retention without objection for an unreasonably long time of a statement of account rendered by the other party is a manifestation of assent.

(2) The account stated does not itself discharge any duty but is an admission by each party of the facts asserted and a promise by the debtor to pay according to its terms.

第 282 条　认可账单

(1) 认可账单，是指债务人和债权人共同作出的、认定记载数额是所欠债权人到期债务的精确计算的同意表示。当事人未经拒绝而在不合理的长期期间保留着对方当事人给付的认可账单的，视为作出了同意表示。

(2) 认可账单本身并不产生任何义务的解除，而是各方当事人对所陈述事实的承认以及债务人根据其条款进行支付的允诺。

TOPIC 3. AGREEMENT OF RESCISSION, RELEASE AND CONTRACT NOT TO SUE

第三节　解约协议、义务免除书和不起诉合同

§ 283. Agreement of Rescission

(1) An agreement of rescission is an agreement under which each party agrees to discharge all of the other party's remaining duties of performance under an existing contract.

(2) An agreement of rescission discharges all remaining duties of performance of both parties. It is a question of interpretation whether the parties also agree to make restitution with respect to performance that has been rendered.

第 283 条　解约协议

(1) 解约协议，是指各方当事人同意解除对方当事人现有合同规定的所有剩余履行义务的协议。

(2) 解约协议解除双方当事人所有剩余的履行义务。当事人是否也同意就已经给付的履行进行返还，是解释问题。

§ 284. Release

(1) A release is a writing providing that a duty owed to the maker of the release is discharged immediately or on the occurrence of a condition.

(2) The release takes effect on delivery as stated in §§ 101–03 and, subject to the occurrence of any condition, discharges the duty.

第 284 条　义务免除书

(1) 义务免除书，是指规定对免除人所负义务马上解除，或者在条件成就时解除的书面文件。

(2) 义务免除书按照第 101～103 条所述规则在交付时生效，并在条件成就时解除义务。

§ 285. Contract Not to Sue

(1) A contract not to sue is a contract under which the obligee of a duty promises never to sue the obligor or a third person to enforce the duty or not to do so for a limited time.

(2) Except as stated in Subsection (3), a contract never to sue discharges the duty and a contract not to sue for a limited time bars an action to enforce the duty during that time.

(3) A contract not to sue one co-obligor bars levy of execution on the property of the promisee during the agreed time but does not bar an action or the recovery of judgment against any co-obligor.

第 285 条 不起诉合同

(1) 不起诉合同，是指义务的权利人允诺永不起诉义务人或者第三人以强制执行该义务，或者在一定期限内不起诉的合同。

(2) 除第 (3) 款所述规则以外，永不起诉合同解除义务，一定期限内不起诉合同阻却在此期间强制执行该义务的诉讼。

(3) 不起诉一位共同义务人的合同，阻却在约定期间内对该受诺人财产的执行，但并不阻却对其他共同义务人的诉讼或者针对其获得有利的判决。

TOPIC 4. ALTERATION
第四节 改动

§ 286. Alteration of Writing

(1) If one to whom a duty is owed under a contract alters a writing that is an integrate agreement or that satisfies the Statute of Frauds with respect to that contract, the duty is discharged if the alteration is fraudulent and material.

(2) An alternation is material if it would, if effective, vary any party's legal relations with the maker of the alteration or adversely affect that party's legal relations

with a third person. The unauthorized insertion in a blank space in a writing is an alteration.

第 286 条　书面文件的改动

（1）合同某项义务的相对人改动了构成完整协议或者满足反欺诈法要求的书面文件的，如果改动是欺诈性的和重大的，该义务解除。

（2）改动如生效会改变任一当事人与改动人的法律关系的，或者对该当事人与第三人的法律关系产生不利影响的，是重大改动。未经授权而在文件空白处填写内容的，是改动。

§ 287. Assent to or Forgiveness of Alteration

（1）If a party, knowing of an alteration that discharges his duty, manifests assent to the altered terms, his manifestation is equivalent to an acceptance of an offer to substitute those terms.

（2）If a party, knowing of an alteration that discharges his duty, asserts a right under the original contract or otherwise manifests a willingness to remain subject to the original contract or to forgive the alteration, the original contract is revived.

第 287 条　同意或者原谅改动

（1）当事人知道导致其义务解除的改动而对改动后的条款表示同意的，视为对提出替代条款的要约表示承诺。

（2）当事人知道导致其义务解除的改动但主张原始合同的权利，或者以其他方式表示愿意继续遵守原始合同，或者对改动表示原谅的，原始合同恢复效力。

第十三章

连带允诺人和受诺人

Chapter 13

JOINT AND SEVERAL
PROMISORS AND PROMISEES

TOPIC 1. JOINT AND SEVERAL PROMISORS
第一节 连带允诺人

§ 288. Promises of the Same Performance

(1) Where two or more parties to a contract make a promise or promises to the same promisee, the manifested intention of the parties determines whether they promise that the same performance or separate performances shall be given.

(2) Unless a contrary intention is manifested, a promise by two or more promisors is a promise that the same performance shall be given.

第288条 允诺同一履行

(1) 两个或者两个以上的合同当事人对同一受诺人作出一个或者多个允诺的，当事人的意思表示决定他们的允诺是给予同一履行还是分别履行。

(2) 除有相反意思表示以外，两个或者两个以上允诺人作出一个允诺的，是允诺给予同一履行。

§ 289. Joint, Several, and Joint and Several Promisors of the Same Performance

(1) Where two or more parties to a contract promise the same performance to the same promisee, each is bound for the whole performance thereof, whether his duty is joint, several, or joint and several.

(2) Where two or more parties to a contract promise the same performance to the same promisee, they incur only a joint duty unless an intention is manifested to create several duties or joint and several duties.

(3) By statute in most states some or all promises which would otherwise create only joint duties create joint and several duties.

第 289 条　同一履行的共同允诺人、单独允诺人和连带允诺人

（1）两个或者两个以上的合同当事人对同一受诺人允诺同一履行的，每人都受到全部履行的约束，无论其义务是共同的、单独的，还是连带的。

（2）两个或者两个以上的合同当事人对同一受诺人允诺同一履行的，除有创设单独义务或者连带义务的意思表示以外，只承担共同义务。

（3）根据大多数州制定法的规定，本来只产生共同义务的某些或者所有允诺产生连带义务。[1]

§ 290. Compulsory Joinder of Joint Promisors

（1）By statute in most states where the distinction between joint duties and joint and several duties retains significance, an action can be maintained against one or more promisors who incur only a joint duty, even though other promisors subject to the same duty are not served with process.

（2）In the absence of statute, an action can be maintained against promisors who incur only a joint duty without joinder of those beyond the jurisdiction of the court, the representatives of deceased promisors, or those against whom the duty is not enforceable at the time of suit.

第 290 条　共同允诺人的强制合并

（1）共同义务与连带义务的区分仍有意义的大多数州的制定法规定，即使承担同一义务的其他允诺人并没有被送达传票，也可以针对只承担共同义务的一个或多个允诺人提起诉讼。

（2）没有制定法的规定时，可以针对只承担共同义务的允诺人提起诉讼，而不能起诉法院管辖权之外的允诺人、已故允诺人的代表人或者起诉时对其承担的义务不可强制执行的允诺人。

---

〔1〕　本款似乎是对现代制定法与传统普通法规则差异的叙述。

§ 291. Judgment in an Action against Co-Promisors

In an action against promisors of the same performance, whether their duties are joint, several, or joint and several, judgment can properly be entered for or against one even though no judgment or a different judgement is entered with respect to another, except that judgment for one and against another is improper where there has been a determination on the merits and the liability of one cannot exist without the liability of the other.

第 291 条　以共同允诺人为被告的诉讼判决

以同一履行的多个允诺人为被告的诉讼中，无论允诺人义务是共同的、单独的还是连带的，都可以适宜地只对一人作出有利或者不利的判决，即使没有针对另一人作出判决，或者针对另一人作出了不同的判决；但如果案件是非曲直已经明了，一人的责任不能独立于对方的责任，因而判决有利于一人而不利于另一人是不适宜的情况除外。

§ 292. Effect of Judgment for or Against Co-Promisors

(1) A judgment against one or more promisors does not discharge other promisors of the same performance unless joinder of the other promisors is required by the rule stated in § 290. By statute in most states judgment against one promisor does not discharge co-promisors even where such joinder is required.

(2) The effect of judgment for one or more promisors of the same performance is determined by the rules of res judicata relating to suretyship or vicarious liability.

第 292 条　对共同允诺人有利或者不利判决的效力

(1) 对一个或者多个允诺人不利的判决并不解除同一履行中其他允诺人的义务，但第 290 条所述规则要求将其他允诺人予以合并的除外。依据大多数州的制定法规定，不利于一个允诺人的判决即使在要求允诺人合并的情况下也不解除共同允诺人的义务。

(2) 有利于同一履行中的一个或者多个允诺人的判决，其效力根据与保证或者转承责任有关的既判力规则决定。

§ 293. Effect of Performance or Satisfaction on Co–Promisors

Full or partial performance or other satisfaction of the contractual duty of a promisor discharges the duty to the obligee of each other promisor of the same performance to the extent of the amount or value applied to the discharge of the duty of the promisor who renders it.

第 293 条　履行或者清偿对共同允诺人的效力

一个允诺人全部或者部分履行，或者以其他形式清偿其合同义务的，在给付履行的允诺人的义务被解除的数量或者价值范围内[1]，同一履行的其他允诺人对于权利人[2]的义务得以解除。

§ 294. Effect of Discharge on Co–Promisors

（1）Except as stated in §295, where the obligee of promises of the same performance discharges one promisor by release, rescission or accord and satisfaction,

（a）co–promisors who are bound only by a joint duty are discharged unless the discharged promisor is a surety for the co–promisor；

（b）co–promisors who are bound by joint and several duties or by several duties are not discharged except to the extent required by the law of suretyship.

（2）By statute in many states a discharge of one promisor does not discharge other promisors of the same performance except to the extent required by the law of suretyship.

（3）Any consideration received by the obligee for discharge of one promisor discharges the duty of each other promisor of the same performance to the extent of the amount or value received. An agreement to the contrary is not effective unless it is made with a surety and expressly preserves the duty of his principal.

---

〔1〕　为了易于理解，译文"在给付履行的允诺人的义务被解除的数量或者价值范围内"的表述视角略有改变；按照原文的视角理解，即为：共同允诺人之一给付履行或者以其他方式清偿合同义务时，该履行或者清偿用于清偿自己的合同义务，且在清偿自己义务的数量或者价值范围内，同一履行的其他共同允诺人的义务也得以解除，即一人履行，众人解除。

〔2〕　权利人（obligee），根据"重述"原文本条评论 b，本条和本章后续条款中的"权利人"一词既包括受诺人，又包括第 302~315 条规定的有权强制执行允诺的受益人。

第 294 条　解除对共同允诺人的效力

（1）除第 295 条所述规则以外，同一履行的允诺的权利人通过义务免除书、解约协议或者和解与清偿解除一个允诺人的义务的，

（a）只受共同义务约束的共同允诺人得以解除义务，但被解除的允诺人是共同允诺人的保证人的除外；

（b）受到连带义务约束或者受到单独义务约束的共同允诺人不能解除，但在保证法要求范围内的除外。

（2）许多州的制定法规定，除保证法要求的以外，一个允诺人的解除并不解除同一履行中的其他允诺人。

（3）权利人收到用以解除一个允诺人义务的对价的，在所收到的数量或者价值范围内，同一履行的每个其他允诺人的义务得以解除。作出相反约定的协议，只有与保证人签订且明确保留主债务人义务时方为有效。

§ 295. Effect of Contract Not to Sue; Reservation of Rights

（1）Where the obligee of promises of the same performance contracts not to sue one promisor, the other promisors are not discharged except to the extent required by the law of suretyship.

（2）Words which purport to release or discharge a promisor and also to reserve rights against other promisors of the same performance have the effect of a contract not to sue rather than a release or discharge.

（3）Any consideration received by the obligee for a contract not to sue one promisor discharges the duty of each other promisor of the same performance to the extent of the amount or value received. An agreement to the contrary is not effective unless it is made with a surety and expressly preserves the duty of his principal.

第 295 条　不起诉合同的效力；权利的保留

（1）同一履行的允诺的权利人约定不起诉一个允诺人的，其他允诺人并不得以解除，但在保证法要求范围内的除外。

（2）宣称免除或者解除某个允诺人的义务并同时保留针对同一履行的其

他允诺人的权利的语词，具有不起诉合同的效力，而非义务免除书或者义务解除的效力。

（3）权利人收到约定不起诉一个允诺人的合同的对价的，同一履行的每个其他允诺人的义务在收到的数量或者价值范围内得以解除。作出相反约定的协议，只有与保证人签订且明确保留主债务人义务时方为有效。

§ 296. Survivorship of Joint Duties

On the death of one of two or more promisors of the same performance in a contract, the estate of the decreased promisor is bound by the contract, whether the duty was joint, several, or joint and several.

第 296 条　共同义务的存续

合同中同一履行的两个或者两个以上允诺人之一死亡的，无论合同义务是共同的、单独的还是连带的性质，已故允诺人的遗产都受到合同的约束。

TOPIC 2.　JOINT AND SEVERAL PROMISEES
第二节　连带受诺人

§ 297. Obligees of the Same Promised Performance

（1）Where a party to a contract makes a promise to two or more promisees or for the benefit of two or more beneficiaries, the manifested intention of the parties determines whether he promises the same performance to all, a separate performance to each, or some combination.

（2）Except to the extent that a different intention is manifested or that the interests of the obligees in the performance or in the remedies for breach are distinct, the rights of obligees of the same performance are joint.

第 297 条　所允诺的同一履行的权利人

（1）合同当事人向两个或者两个以上的受诺人作出允诺，或者为了两个或者两个以上的受益人的利益作出允诺的，各方当事人的意思表示决定他对所有人允诺了同一履行，对每人允诺了各自独立的履行，还是两者的某种组合。

（2）除有不同的意思表示，或者权利人在履行或违约救济方面的权益明显不同以外，同一履行的权利人的权利是共同的。

§ 298. Compulsory Joinder of Joint Obligees

（1）In an action based on a joint right created by a promise, the promisor by making appropriate objection can prevent recovery of judgment against him unless there are joined either as plaintiffs or as defendants all the surviving joint obligees.

（2）Except in actions on negotiable instruments and except as stated in §300, any joint obligee unless limited by agreement may sue in the name of all the joint obligees for the enforcement of the promise by a money judgment.

第298条 共同权利人的强制共同诉讼

（1）在基于允诺产生的共同权利的诉讼中，除所有存续的共同权利人都合并为原告或者被告以外，允诺人作出适宜的反对即可阻止对自己不利的判决。

（2）除有关流通票据的诉讼以及第300条所述规则以外，若无协议限制，任何共同权利人都可以以所有共同权利人的名义起诉，要求以金钱判决的形式强制执行允诺。

§ 299. Discharge by or Tender to One Joint Obligee

Except where the promise is made in a negotiable instrument and except as stated in §300, any joint obligee, unless limited by agreement, has power to discharge the promisor by receipt of the promised performance or by release or otherwise, and tender to one joint obligee is equivalent to a tender to all.

第299条 共同权利人之一解除义务或者向其提交履行

除在可流通票据中作出的允诺以及第300条所述规则以外，若非受到协议限制，任何共同权利人都有权在收到所允诺的履行后，或者通过义务免除书或者以其他方式，解除允诺人的义务，且向一个共同权利人提交履行等同于向所有共同权利人提交。

§ 300. Effect of Violation of Duty to a Co-Obligee

（1）If an obligee attempts or threatens to discharge the promisor in violation of his duty to a co-obligee of the same performance, the co-obligee may obtain an injunction forbidding the discharge.

（2）A discharge of the promisor by an obligee in violation of his duty to a co-obligee of the same performance is voidable to the extent necessary to protect the co-obligee's interest in the performance, except to the extent that the promisor has given value or otherwise changed his position in good faith and without knowledge or reason to know of the violation.

第 300 条　违反对共同权利人承担的义务的效力

（1）权利人违反对同一履行的共同权利人承担的义务而意图解除或者威胁解除允诺人的义务的，共同权利人可以获得禁止令对解除行为予以禁止。

（2）权利人违反对同一履行的共同权利人承担的义务而解除允诺人义务的，在保护共同权利人在履行中的权益所必需的范围内，解除是可撤销的，但允诺人为善意且在不知道或者没有理由知道权利人违反义务的情况下给付了对价，或者在其他方面改变了地位的除外。

§ 301. Survivorship of Joint Rights

On the death of a joint obligee, unless a contrary intention was manifested, the surviving obligees are solely entitled as against the promisor to receive performance, to discharge the promisor, or to sue for the enforcement of the promise by a money judgment. On the death of the last surviving obligee, only his estate is so entitled.

第 301 条　共同权利的存续

共同权利人死亡的，除有相反意思表示的以外，生存的权利人具有受领履行、解除允诺人义务或者诉请金钱判决以执行允诺的针对允诺人的专属权利。最后一个权利人死亡的，只有最后死亡的权利人的遗产获得此权利。

第十四章

合同受益人

Chapter 14

CONTRACT BENEFICIARIES

§ 302. Intended and Incidental Beneficiaries

（1）Unless otherwise agreed between promisor and promisee, a beneficiary of a promise is an intended beneficiary if recognition of a right to performance in the beneficiary is appropriate to effectuate the intention of the parties and either

（a）the performance of the promise will satisfy an obligation of the promisee to pay money to the beneficiary; or

（b）the circumstances indicate that the promisee intends to give the beneficiary the benefit of the promised performance.

（2）An incidental beneficiary is a beneficiary who is not an intended beneficiary.

第302条　目标受益人与附带受益人

（1）除允诺人与受诺人另有约定以外，如果认可允诺的受益人对于履行享有权利，可以适宜地实现当事人的意图且有下列情形的，该受益人是目标受益人：

（a）允诺的履行将清偿受诺人向受益人支付金钱的义务的；或者

（b）情形表明，受诺人有给予受益人所允诺的履行利益的意图的。

（2）附带受益人，是指不是目标受益人的受益人。

§ 303. Conditional Promises; Promises Under Seal

The statements in this Chapter are applicable to both conditional and unconditional promises and to sealed and unsealed promises.

第303条　附条件的允诺；盖印允诺

本章所述规则同时适用于附条件的允诺和无条件的允诺，盖印的允诺和非盖印的允诺。

§ 304. Creation of Duty to Beneficiary

A promise in a contract creates a duty in the promisor to any intended beneficiary to perform the promise, and the intended beneficiary may enforce the duty.

第 304 条 创设对受益人的义务

合同中的允诺创设了允诺人对目标受益人履行允诺的义务，且目标受益人可以强制执行该义务。

§ 305. Overlapping Duties to Beneficiary and Promisee

(1) A promise in a contract creates a duty in the promisor to the promisee to perform the promise even though he also has a similar duty to an intended beneficiary.

(2) Whole or partial satisfaction of the promisor's duty to the beneficiary satisfies to that extent the promisor's duty to the promisee.

第 305 条 对受益人和受诺人所承担义务的重合

(1) 合同中的允诺创设了允诺人对受诺人履行允诺的义务，即使允诺人对目标受益人也负有类似义务。

(2) 允诺人对受益人的义务已经全部或者部分清偿的，允诺人对受诺人的义务在此范围内也得以清偿。

§ 306. Disclaimer by a Beneficiary

A beneficiary who has not previously assented to the promise for his benefit may in a reasonable time after learning of its existence and terms render any duty to himself inoperative from the beginning by disclaimer.

第 306 条 受益人的弃权

受益人事先并没有对使其受益的允诺表示同意的，可以在得知这一允诺及其条款之后的合理时间内，通过弃权而使得自己负有的任何义务自始不产生效力。

§ 307. Remedy of Specific Performance

Where specific performance is otherwise an appropriate remedy, either the promisee or the beneficiary may maintain a suit for specific enforcement of a duty owed to an intended beneficiary.

第 307 条　具体履行救济

具体履行救济在其他方面都适当的，受诺人或者受益人均可以维持对目标受益人所负义务强制执行的诉讼。

§ 308. Identification of Beneficiaries

It is not essential to the creation of a right in an intended beneficiary that he be identified when a contract containing the promise is made.

第 308 条　受益人的确定

目标受益人权利的创设，并不以包含允诺的合同订立时目标受益人的确定为必需。

§ 309. Defenses Against the Beneficiary

（1）A promise creates no duty to a beneficiary unless a contract is formed between the promisor and the promisee; and if a contract is voidable or unenforceable at the time of its formation the right of any beneficiary is subject to the infirmity.

（2）If a contract ceases to be binding in whole or in part because of impracticability, public policy, non-occurrence of a condition, or present or prospective failure of performance, the right of any beneficiary is to that extent discharged or modified.

（3）Except as stated in Subsections（1）and（2）and in § 311 or as provided by the contract, the right of any beneficiary against the promisor is not subject to the promisor's claims or defenses against the promisee or to the promisee's claims or defenses against the beneficiary.

（4）A beneficiary's right against the promisor is subject to any claim or defense arising from his own conduct or agreement.

第 309 条　对受益人的抗辩

（1）除允诺人与受诺人之间订立合同的以外，允诺不创设对受益人的义务；合同在订立时是可撤销的或者不可强制执行的，受益人的权利也受该缺陷的限制。

（2）由于履行不能、公共政策、条件不成就或者当前或预期不履行，因而导致合同全部或部分失去约束力的，任何受益人的权利在此范围内被解除或者变更。

（3）除第（1）款、第（2）款以及第 311 条所述规则或者合同约定以外，任何受益人针对允诺人的权利并不受允诺人对受诺人的主张或者抗辩的限制，也不受受诺人针对受益人的主张或者抗辩的限制。

（4）受益人针对允诺人的权利，受到源自自己的行为或者协议的任何主张或者抗辩的限制。

§ 310. Remedies of the Beneficiary of a Promise to Pay the Promisee's Debt; Reimbursement of Promisee

（1）Where an intended beneficiary has an enforceable claim against the promisee, he can obtain a judgment or judgments against either the promisee or the promisor or both based on their respective duties to him. Satisfaction in whole or in part of either of these duties, or of a judgment thereon, satisfies to that extent the other duty or judgment, subject to the promisee's right of subrogation.

（2）To the extent that the claim of an intended beneficiary is satisfied from assets of the promisee, the promisee has a right of reimbursement from the promisor, which may be enforced directly and also, if the beneficiary's claim is fully satisfied, by subrogation to the claim of the beneficiary against the promisor, and to any judgment thereon and to any security therefor.

第 310 条　替受诺人偿债的允诺中受益人的救济；受诺人索偿

（1）目标受益人拥有针对受诺人的可强制执行的主张的，可以针对受诺人、允诺人或者受诺人允诺人双方，以他们对自己所负的相应义务为基础获得判决。其中任一义务或者任一判决全部或者部分清偿的，在符合受诺人代位权的条件下，另一义务或者判决在此范围内得以清偿。

（2）在目标受益人的主张已经由受诺人的资产清偿的范围内，受诺人有权向允诺人索偿，索偿可以直接强制执行；受益人的主张已经全部清偿的，也可以由受诺人代位取得受益人对允诺人的主张、任何有关判决以及任何为此目的的抵押。

§ 311. Variation of a Duty to a Beneficiary

（1）Discharge or modification of a duty to an intended beneficiary by conduct of the promisee or by a subsequent agreement between promisor and promisee is ineffective if a term of the promise creating the duty so provides.

（2）In the absence of such a term, the promisor and promisee retain power to discharge or modify the duty by subsequent agreement.

（3）Such a power terminates when the beneficiary, before he receives notification of the discharge or modification, materially changes his position in justifiable reliance on the promise or brings suit on it or manifests assent to it at the request of the promisor or promisee.

（4）If the promisee receives consideration for an attempted discharge or modification of the promisor's duty which is ineffective against the beneficiary, the beneficiary can assert a right to the consideration so received. The promisor's duty is discharged to the extent of the amount received by the beneficiary.

第 311 条　改变对受益人所承担的义务

（1）通过受诺人的行为或者允诺人与受诺人随后的协议解除或者变更对目标受益人承担的义务的，如果创设该义务的允诺条款规定此种解除或者变更无效，则解除或者变更无效。

（2）允诺中没有包含此种条款的，允诺人和受诺人保留通过事后协议解除或者变更该义务的权利。

（3）受益人收到解除或者变更通知之前，因合理信赖允诺而实质性地改变了地位，或者针对允诺提起了诉讼，或者应允诺人或者受诺人的请求对允诺表示了同意的，允诺人和受诺人的这一权利终止。

（4）受诺人收到为试图解除或者变更允诺人的义务而支付的对价的，如果该解除或者变更对受益人无效，受益人可以对受诺人收到的对价主张权利。允诺人的义务在受益人所收数额范围内解除。

§ 312. Mistakes as to Duty to Beneficiary

The effect of an erroneous belief of the promisor or promisee as to the existence or extent of a duty owed to an intended beneficiary is determined by the rules making contracts voidable for mistake.

第 312 条　有关对受益人所负义务的错误

允诺人或者受诺人对于向目标受益人所负义务存在与否或者义务范围有错误认识的，认识的效力根据因错误而撤销合同的规则确定。

§ 313. Government Contracts

（1）The rules stated in this Chapter apply to contracts with a government or governmental agency except to the extent that application would contravene the policy of the law authorizing the contract or prescribing remedies for its breach.

（2）In particular, a promisor who contracts with a government or governmental agency to do an act for or render a service to the public is not subject to contractual liability to a member of the public for consequential damages resulting from performance or failure to perform unless

（a）the terms of the promise provide for such liability; or

（b）the promisee is subject to liability to the member of the public for the damages and a direct action against the promisor is consistent with the terms of the contract and with the policy of the law authorizing the contract and prescribing remedies for its breach.

第 313 条　政府合同

（1）本章所述规则适用于与政府或者政府代理人订立的合同，但违背授权合同订立的法律的政策，或者违背规定违约救济的法律的政策的除外。

（2）特别而言，允诺人与政府或者政府代理人订立合同，约定为公众从事行为或者向公众提供服务的，除下列情形以外，并不因履行或者未履行而导致的后果性损害[1]向公众成员承担合同责任：

（a）允诺条款规定了这种责任的；或者

（b）受诺人向公众成员承担着损害赔偿责任，且对允诺人直接提起诉讼与合同条款一致，也与授权合同订立和规定违约救济的法律的政策一致的。

§ 314. Suretyship Defenses

An intended beneficiary who has an enforceable claim against the promisee is affected by the incidents of the suretyship of the promisee from the time he has knowledge of it.

第314条　保证关系抗辩

对受诺人存在可强制执行主张的目标受益人，自得知受诺人的保证关系之时起，受到受诺人保证关系事件的影响。

§ 315. Effect of a Promise of Incidental Benefit

An incidental beneficiary acquires by virtue of the promise no right against the promisor or the promisee.

第315条　允诺附带利益的效力

附带受益人不因允诺而获得针对允诺人或者受诺人的权利。

---

[1] 后果性损害（consequential damages），consequential damages 经常被译为"后果性损害赔偿""间接损害赔偿"，但此处采取直译，并根据上下文进行了适当调整。

第十五章

权利转让与义务转托

Chapter 15

ASSIGNMENT AND
DELEGATION

§ 316. Scope of This Chapter

（1）In this Chapter, references to assignment of a right or delegation of a duty or condition, to the obligee or obligor of an assigned right or delegated duty, or to an assignor or assignee, are limited to rights, duties, and conditions arising under a contract or for breach of a contract.

（2）The statements in this Chapter are qualified in some respects by statutory and other rules governing negotiable instruments and documents, relating to interests in land, and affecting other classes of contracts.

第 316 条　本章范围

（1）本章指称权利转让或者义务或条件的转托，被转让的权利或者转托的义务的权利人或义务人，或者转让人或受让人时，都限于源自合同的或者因违反合同而产生的权利、义务和条件。

（2）本章所述规则在某些方面受到调整流通票据和单据的、与土地权益相关的以及影响其他合同类型的制定法和其他规则的限定。

TOPIC 1. WHAT CAN BE ASSIGNED OR DELEGATED
第一节　什么可以转让或者转托

§ 317. Assignment of a Right

（1）An assignment of a right is a manifestation of the assignor's intention to transfer it by virtue of which the assignor's right to performance by the obligor is extinguished in whole or in part and the assignee acquires a right to such performance.

（2）A contractual right can be assigned unless

（a）the substitution of a right of the assignee for the right of the assignor would materially change the duty of the obligor, or materially increase the burden or risk imposed on him by his contract, or materially impair his chance of obtaining return performance, or materially reduce its value to him, or

(b) the assignment is forbidden by statute or is otherwise inoperative on grounds of public policy, or

(c) assignment is validly precluded by contract.

第 317 条　权利的转让

（1）权利的转让，是指转让人愿意转移权利，因而其享有的对义务人履行的权利全部或部分消灭，而受让人获得对该履行的权利的意思表示。

（2）除下列情形以外，合同权利可以转让：

（a）将转让人的权利替换为受让人的权利将实质性地改变义务人的义务，或者实质性地增加义务人的合同带给他的负担或风险，或者实质性地损害义务人获得回报履行的机会，或者实质性地降低回报履行的价值的，或者

（b）转让被制定法所禁止，或者在其他方面由于公共政策而不能实行的，或者

（c）转让被合同有效禁止的。

§ 318. Delegation of Performance of Duty

（1）An obligor can properly delegate the performance of his duty to another unless the delegation is contrary to public policy or the terms of his promise.

（2）Unless otherwise agreed, a promise requires performance by a particular person only to the extent that the obligee has a substantial interest in having that person perform or control the acts promised.

（3）Unless the obligee agrees otherwise, neither delegation of performance nor a contract to assume the duty made with the obligor by the person delegated discharges any duty or liability of the delegating obligor.

第 318 条　义务履行的转托

（1）义务人可以适宜地将自己的履行义务转托他人，但转托与公共政策或者义务人的允诺条款相悖的除外。

（2）除另有约定以外，只有权利人对由特定人履行或者控制所允诺的行为具有实质性权益时，允诺才可以要求特定人履行。

（3）除权利人另行同意以外，无论履行的转托还是与义务人订立的被转托人承担义务的合同，都不能解除转托义务人的任何义务或者责任。

§ 319. Delegation of Performance of Condition

（1）Where a performance by a person is made a condition of a duty, performance by a person delegated by him satisfies that requirement unless the delegation is contrary to public policy or the terms of the agreement.

（2）Unless otherwise agreed, an agreement requires performance of a condition by a particular person only to the extent that the obligor has a substantial interest in having that person perform or control the acts required.

第319条 条件履行的转托

（1）某人的履行是义务的条件的，由该人转托的人履行也满足这一要求，但转托与公共政策或者协议条款相悖的除外。

（2）除另有约定以外，只有义务人对由特定人履行或者控制所要求的行为具有实质性权益时，协议才构成要求特定人履行的条件。

§ 320. Assignment of Conditional Rights

The fact that a right is created by an option contract or is conditional on the performance of a return promise or is otherwise conditional does not prevent its assignment before the condition occurs.

第320条 附条件权利的转让

权利由选择权合同创设，以回报允诺的履行为条件，或者附属于其他条件的，不阻却条件成就之前的转让。

§ 321. Assignment of Future Rights

（1）Except as otherwise provided by statute, an assignment of a right to payment expected to arise out of an existing employment or other continuing business re-lationship is effective in the same way as an assignment of an existing right.

(2) Except as otherwise provided by statute and as stated in Subsection (1), a purported assignment of a right expected to arise under a contract not in existence op-erates only as a promise to assign the right when it arises and as a power to enforce it.

第321条　未来权利的转让

(1) 若非制定法另行规定，转让源自现存雇佣关系或者其他持续性商务关系的期待性支付权利的，其效力同转让既存权利。

(2) 除制定法另行规定以及第（1）款所述规则以外，对尚不存在的合同项下的期待权利宣称进行转让的，只是对权利产生时进行转让的允诺和对该允诺的强制执行权的授予。

§ 322. Contractual Prohibition of Assignment

(1) Unless the circumstances indicate the contrary, a contract term prohibiting assignment of "the contract" bars only the delegation to an assignee of the perform-ance by the assignor of a duty or condition.

(2) A contract term prohibiting assignment of rights under the contract, unless a different intention is manifested,

(a) does not forbid assignment of a right to damages for breach of the whole contract or a right arising out of the assignor's due performance of his entire obliga-tion;

(b) gives the obligor a right to damages for breach of the terms forbidding as-signment but does not render the assignment ineffective;

(c) is for the benefit of the obligor, and does not prevent the assignee from ac-quiring rights against the assignor or the obligor from discharging his duty as if there were no such prohibition.

第322条　合同对转让的禁止

(1) 除情形有相反表示的以外，合同条款禁止转让"合同"的，只是阻却转让人将义务履行或者条件履行转托给受让人。

（2）除有不同意思表示的以外，合同条款禁止转让合同权利的，

（a）并不禁止转让因违反整个合同而产生的获得损害赔偿金的权利，或者因转让人适当履行全部义务而产生的权利；

（b）赋予义务人在对方违反禁止转让条款时获得损害赔偿金的权利，但并不导致转让不产生效力；

（c）是为保护义务人的利益，并不阻却受让人取得针对转让人的权利，也不阻止义务人义务的解除，如同禁止条款并不存在。

§ 323. Obligor's Assent to Assignment or Delegation

（1）A term of a contract manifesting an obligor's assent to the future assignment of a right or an obligee's assent to the future delegation of the performance of a duty or condition is effective despite any subsequent objection.

（2）A manifestation of such assent after the formation of a contract is similarly effective if made for consideration or in circumstances in which a promise would be binding without consideration, or if a material change of position takes place in reliance on the manifestation.

第 323 条 义务人对转让或者转托的同意

（1）按照合同条款的表示，义务人同意将来转让权利的，或者权利人同意将来转托义务或者条件的履行的，即使事后反对，合同条款也有效。

（2）上述同意表示是为了对价作出的，或者没有对价的允诺也会产生约束力的，或者因信赖同意表示而产生地位的重大改变的，合同订立之后作出的同意表示同样有效。

TOPIC 2. MODE OF ASSIGNMENT OR DELEGATION
第二节　权利转让或者义务转托的方式

§ 324. Mode of Assignment in General

It is essential to an assignment of a right that the obligee manifest an intention to transfer the right to another person without further action or manifestation of intention by the obligee. The manifestation may be made to the other or to a third person on his behalf and, except as provided by statute or by contract, may be made either orally or by a writing.

第 324 条　转让方式的一般规则

转让权利的，必须由权利人作出向他人转让权利的意思表示，但无需权利人再采取其他行为或者作出其他意思表示。意思表示可以向对方作出，也可以向代表对方的第三人作出；除非制定法或者合同另有规定，否则既可以采用口头形式，也可以采用书面形式。

§ 325. Order as Assignment

(1) A written order drawn upon an obligor and signed and delivered to another person by the obligee is an assignment if it is conditional on the existence of a duty of the drawee to the drawer to comply with the order and the drawer manifests an intention that a person other than the drawer is to retain the performance.

(2) An order which directs the drawee to render a performance without reference to any duty of the drawee is not of itself an assignment, even though the drawee is under a duty to the drawer to comply with the order and even though the order indicates a particular account to be debited or any other fund or source from which reimbursement is expected.

第 325 条　付款指示作为转让

(1) 从义务人处支取款项的书面付款指示，经权利人签字后向他人交付的，如果以存在付款人遵守出票人指示的义务为条件，且出票人作出了由出票人以外的人保留履行的意思表示，则书面付款指示即为权利转让。

（2）即使付款人对出票人负有遵守指示的义务，甚至即使付款指示载有具体借记账户或者用于偿付的其他资金或者来源，只是指令付款人给付履行但并未提及付款人任何义务的，付款指示并不自然构成权利转让。

§ 326. Partial Assignment

（1）Except as stated in Subsection（2）, an assignment of a part of a right, whether the part is specified as a fraction, as an amount, or otherwise, is operative as to that part to the same extent and in the same manner as if the part had been a separate right.

（2）If the obligor has not contracted to perform separately the assigned part of a right, no legal proceeding can be maintained by the assignor or assignee against the obligor over his objection, unless all the persons entitled to the promised performance are joined in the proceeding, or unless joinder is not feasible and it is equitable to proceed without joinder.

第 326 条　部分转让

（1）除了第（2）款所述规则以外，对权利进行部分转让的，无论部分权利是以比例、数量还是其他形式描述，其转让的范围和方式都与该部分权利是独立权利时相同。

（2）义务人尚无合同义务单独履行权利的被转让部分的，转让人或者受让人不能因义务人的拒绝而提起法律程序，但对允诺的履行有权利的人全部加入法律程序的，或者诉讼合并不现实且不经合并而继续进行诉讼是公平的除外。

§ 327. Acceptance or Disclaimer by the Assignee

（1）A manifestation of assent by an assignee to the assignment is essential to make it effective unless

（a）a third person gives consideration for the assignment, or （b）the assignment is irrevocable by virtue of the delivery of a writing to a third person.

（2）An assignee who has not manifested assent to an assignment may, within a reasonable time after learning of its existence and terms, render it inoperative from the beginning by disclaimer.

第 327 条　受让人的接受或者弃权

（1）除下列情形以外，转让生效必须经受让人作出同意表示：

（a）第三人支付了转让对价的，或者

（b）由于向第三人交付了书面文件因而转让是不可撤销的。

（2）受让人尚未对转让作出同意表示的，可以在得知转让以及转让条款之后的合理期间内通过弃权使得转让自始不产生效力。

§ 328. Interpretation of Words of Assignment; Effect of Acceptance of Assignment

（1）Unless the language or the circumstances indicate the contrary, as in an assignment for security, an assignment of "the contract" or of "all my rights under the contract" or an assignment in similar general terms is an assignment of the assignor's rights and a delegation of his unperformed duties under the contract.

（2）Unless the language or the circumstances indicate the contrary, the acceptance by an assignee operates as a promise to the assignor to perform the assignor's unperformed duties, and the obligor of the assigned rights is an intended beneficiary of the promise.

Caveat: The Institute expresses no opinion as to whether the rule stated in Subsection（2）applies to an assignment by a purchaser of his rights under a contract for the sale of land.

第328条　转让的语词解释；接受转让的效力

（1）除语言或者情形有相反表示的（例如为担保进行的转让）〔1〕以外，对"本合同"或者"本合同项下的我方所有权利"的转让，或者类似的宽泛语词表述的转让，是对转让人合同项下权利的转让和未履行义务的转托。

（2）除语言或者情形有相反表示的以外，受让人对转让表示接受的，是向转让人允诺履行转让人未履行的义务，被转让权利的义务人是允诺的目标受益人。

注意：至于第（2）款所述规则是否适用于土地销售合同项下买受人权利的转让，美国法学会不发表意见。

§ 329. Repudiation by Assignor and Novation with Assignee

（1）The legal effect of a repudiation by an assignor of his duty to the obligor of the assigned right is not limited by the fact that the assignee is a competent person and has promised to perform the duty.

（2）If the obligor, with knowledge of such a repudiation, accepts any performance from the assignee without reserving his rights against the assignor, a novation arises by which the duty of the assignor is discharged and a similar duty of the assignee is substituted.

第329条　权利转让人拒绝履行与受让人的更新

（1）转让人拒绝履行对被转让权利的义务人负有的义务的，拒绝履行的效力不受受让人具有能力且已经作出履行义务的允诺这一事实的限制。

（2）在知道拒绝履行的情况下，义务人接受了受让人的履行且未保留对抗转让人的权利的，合同得以更新，转让人的义务解除，并替换为受让人的相似义务。

---

〔1〕　除语言或者情形有相反表示的（例如为担保进行的转让）（Unless the language or the circumstances indicate the contrary, as in an assignment for security），原文的含义是，以担保为目的的转让一般不会由被担保人承担转让人的义务。

§ 330. Contracts to Assign in the Future, or to Transfer Proceeds to be Received

(1) A contract to make a future assignment of a right, or to transfer proceeds to be received in the future by the promisor, is not an assignment.

(2) Except as provided by statute, the effect of such a contract on the rights and duties of the obligor and third persons is determined by the rules relating to specific performance of contracts.

第330条 约定将来转让权利或者转让未来的收益

(1) 合同约定将来转让权利的，或者转让允诺人将来获得的收益的，不是权利转让。

(2) 除制定法的规定以外，这种合同对于义务人和第三人的权利义务的效力，根据关于合同具体履行的规则确定。

TOPIC 3. EFFECT BETWEEN ASSIGNOR AND ASSIGNEE
第三节 转让人与受让人之间的效力

§ 331. Partially Effective Assignments

An assignment may be conditional, revocable, or voidable by the assignor, or unenforceable by virtue of a Statute of Frauds.

第331条 部分有效的转让

转让可以是附条件的、可撤销的或者转让人可撤销的[1]，或者是因违反

---

[1] 本条翻译的字面包含两个"可撤销"，"可撤销的"对应 revocable，"转让人可撤销的"对应 voidable。前者指先前授予了权利，此后又将权利收回，在本语境中可以指撤销转让允诺，原因可包括转让是无偿的（参阅第332条），或者转让人保留了撤销的权利。后者所适用的语境主要是合同成立后由于某些无效事由（如缺乏行为能力、存在欺诈等）而可以由撤销权人撤销（当然也可以追认）。参见张法连（2014）、"重述"原文本条评论 a 以及其他有关著述。

反欺诈法而不可强制执行的。

§ 332. Revocability of Gratuitous Assignments

（1）Unless a contrary intention is manifested, a gratuitous assignment is irrevocable if

（a）the assignment is in a writing either signed or under seal that is delivered by the assignor; or

（b）the assignment is accompanied by delivery of a writing of a type customarily accepted as a symbol or as evidence of the right assigned.

（2）Except as stated in this Section, a gratuitous assignment is revocable and the right of the assignee is terminated by the assignor's death or incapacity, by a subsequent assignment by the assignor, or by notification from the assignor received by the assignee or by the obligor.

（3）A gratuitous assignment ceases to be revocable to the extent that before the assignee's right is terminated he obtains

（a）payment or satisfaction of the obligations, or

（b）judgment against the obligor, or

（c）a new contract of the obligor by novation.

（4）A gratuitous assignment is irrevocable to the extent necessary to avoid injustice where the assignor should reasonably expect the assignment to induce action or forbearance by the assignee or a sub-assignee and the assignment does induce such action or forbearance.

（5）An assignment is gratuitous unless it is given or taken

（a）in exchange for a performance or return promise that would be consideration for a promise; or

（b）as security for or in total or partial satisfaction of a pre-existing debt or other obligation.

第 332 条　赠与性转让的可撤销性

（1）除有相反意思表示的以外，赠与性转让有下列情形时是不可撤销的：

（a）转让以书面形式作出，且经签字或者盖印后由转让人交付的；或者

（b）转让伴随着通常被视为被转让权利的象征或者证据的文件交付的。

（2）除本条所述规则以外，赠与性转让是可以撤销的；转让人死亡或者丧失行为能力的，转让人随后又进行了转让的，或者经转让人通知且受让人或者义务人收到通知的，受让人的权利终止。

（3）受让人在权利终止之前有下列情形的，赠与性转让不再可以撤销：

（a）受领了付款或者义务的清偿的，或者

（b）获得了针对义务人的判决的，或者

（c）通过更新获得了义务人的新合同的。

（4）转让人能够合理预见，转让会诱使受让人或者次受让人的行为或者不行为，且确实诱使了行为或者不行为发生的，在避免不公正所必需的范围内，赠与性转让是不可撤销的。

（5）除下列情形以外的转让是赠与性的：

（a）权利的给予或者接受是为了交换构成允诺的对价的履行或者回报允诺的；或者

（b）权利的给予或者接受是为先前之债或者其他债务提供担保，或者进行全部或者部分清偿的。

§ 333. Warranties of an Assignor

（1）Unless a contrary intention is manifested, one who assigns or purports to assign a right by assignment under seal or for value warrants to the assignee

（a）that he will do nothing to defeat or impair the value of the assignment and has no knowledge of any fact which would do so;

（b）that the right, as assigned, actually exists and is subject to no limitations or defenses good against the assignor other than those stated or apparent at the time of the assignment;

（c）that any writing evidencing the right which is delivered to the assignee or exhibited to him to induce him to accept the assignment is genuine and what it purports to be.

（2）An assignment does not of itself operate as a warranty that the obligor is solvent or that he will perform his obligation.

（3）An assignor is bound by affirmations and promises to the assignee with ref-erence to the right assigned in the same way and to the same extent that one who transfers goods is bound in like circumstances.

（4）An assignment of a right to a sub-assignee does not operate as an assign-ment of the assignee's right under his assignor's warranties unless an intention is manifested to assign the rights under the warranties.

第 333 条　转让人的保证

（1）除有相反意思表示的以外，转让人以盖印或者有偿方式转让或者宣称转让权利的，是对转让人作出如下保证[1]：

（a）转让人将不从事任何毁坏或有损被转让权利的价值的行为，并且不知道存在会产生这种损害的事实；

（b）被转让的权利是实际存在的，且除转让之时已经说明的或者显而易见的限制、抗辩之外，不存在任何针对转让人的有效限制或者抗辩。

（c）已经交付受让人或者向受让人出示的、诱使其接受转让的任何书面权利证明文件都是真实的，且与文件宣称的内容一致。

（2）转让并不当然是义务人有偿付能力或者将会履行义务的保证。

（3）转让人受到他就被转让权利向受让人所作的真实性确认[2]和允诺的约束，约束方式和范围与货物转让人在同类情形下所受约束相同。

（4）将权利转让给次受让人的，受让人的权利转让并不附带转让人的保证，但有附带这种保证的意思表示的除外。

----

[1]　保证（warranty 或者 warrant），此处是指瑕疵担保意义上的"保证"。请比较第 251 条、第 88 条注释。

[2]　真实性确认（affirmation），根据《元照英美法词典》的译名"确认"定名，指"一种正式的陈述或声明，用以担保宣誓书（affidavit）的内容或证人的证词是真实的。在某些情况下，用这种形式来代替宣誓"（薛波 2003：48）。

TOPIC 4. EFFECT ON THE OBLIGOR'S DUTY
第四节　对义务人义务的效力

§ 334. Variation of Obligor's Duty by Assignment

(1) If the obligor's duty is conditional on the personal cooperation of the original obligee or another person, an assignee's right is subject to the same condition.

(2) If the obligor's duty is conditional on cooperation which the obligee could properly delegate to an agent, the condition may occur if there is similar cooperation by an assignee.

第 334 条　转让对义务人义务的改变

(1) 义务人的义务以原始权利人或者他人的个人配合为条件的，受让人的权利受到相同条件的制约。

(2) 义务人的义务以权利人可以适宜地转托代理人提供的合作为条件的，如果存在受让人提供的类似合作，则条件可以成就。

§ 335. Assignment by a Joint Obligee

A joint obligee may effectively assign his right, but the assignee can enforce it only in the same manner and to the same extent as the assignor could have enforced it.

第 335 条　共同权利人的转让

共同权利人可以有效地转让其权利，但受让人强制执行权利的方式和范围只能与转让人相同。

§ 336. Defenses Against an Assignee

(1) By an assignment the assignee acquires a right against the obligor only to the extent that the obligor is under a duty to the assignor; and if the right of the assignor would be voidable by the obligor or unenforceable against him if no assignment

had been made, the right of the assignee is subject to the infirmity.

(2) The right of an assignee is subject to any defense or claim of the obligor which accrues before the obligor receives notification of the assignment, but not to defenses or claims which accrue thereafter except as stated in this Section or as provided by statute.

(3) Where the right of an assignor is subject to discharge or modification in whole or in part by impracticability, public policy, non-occurrence of a condition, or present or prospective failure of performance by an obligee, the right of the assignee is to that extent subject to discharge or modification even after the obligor receives notification of the assignment.

(4) An assignee's right against the obligor is subject to any defense or claim arising from his conduct or to which he was subject as a party or a prior assignee because he had notice.

第 336 条 对受让人的抗辩

(1) 受让人通过权利转让取得针对义务人的权利，但只限于义务人对转让人所负义务的范围之内；如果不发生转让时转让人的权利可以由义务人撤销的，或者不可以对义务人强制执行的，受让人的权利也受该缺陷的限制。

(2) 受让人的权利受到义务人收到转让通知之前产生的抗辩或者主张的限制，但除本条所述规则或者制定法另有规定以外，不受转让通知之后产生的抗辩或者主张的限制。

(3) 转让人的权利由于履行不能、公共政策、条件不成就或者权利人当前或预期不履行而受到全部或部分解除、变更的限制的，即使在义务人收到转让通知之后，受让人的权利也在此范围内受到解除或者变更的限制。

(4) 受让人针对义务人的权利，受到受让人自身行为产生的抗辩或主张的限制，或者受让人作为当事人或先前受让人由于知悉[1]而曾经受到限制的抗辩或主张的限制。

---

[1] 知悉 (notice) 是指某人已经获得通知的状况，因而有理由知道，实际上并不一定知道，而 knowledge 意为"明知"，即事实上的知道 (薛波 2003：981)。本书中将"knowledge"或者"know"等译为"知道"，为"明知"之意，与"知悉"相对照。

§ 337. Elimination of Defenses by Subsequent Events

Where the right of an assignor is limited or voidable or unenforceable or subject to discharge or modification, subsequent events which would eliminate the limitation or defense have the same effect on the right of the assignee.

第 337 条　继发事件导致抗辩消灭

转让人的权利是受限的、可撤销的、不可强制执行的或者受到解除或变更的限制的，随后发生的会消灭这些限制或者抗辩的事件对受让人的权利具有相同效力。

§ 338. Discharge of an Obligor After Assignment

(1) Except as stated in this Section, notwithstanding an assignment, the assignor retains his power to discharge or modify the duty of the obligor to the extent that the obligor performs or otherwise gives value until but not after the obligor receives notification that the right has been assigned and that performance is to be rendered to the assignee.

(2) So far as an assigned right is conditional on the performance of a return promise, and notwithstanding notification of the assignment, any notification of or substitution for the contract made by the assignor and obligor in good faith and in accordance with reasonable commercial standards is effective against the assignee. The assignee acquires corresponding rights under the modified or substituted contract.

(3) Notwithstanding a defect in the right of an assignee, he has the same power his assignor had to discharge or modify the duty of the obligor to the extent that the obligor gives value or otherwise changes his position in good faith and without knowledge or reason to know the defect.

(4) Where there is a writing of a type customarily accepted as a symbol or as evidence of the right assigned, a discharge or modification is not effective

(a) against the owner or an assignor having a power of avoidance, unless given by him or by a person in possession of the writing with his consent and any necessary endorsement or assignment;

（b）against a subsequent assignee who takes possession of the writing and gives value in good faith and without knowledge or reason to know of the discharge or modification.

第338条 转让之后解除义务人的义务

（1）除本条所述规则以外，尽管存在转让，转让人在义务人履行或者以其他方式给付对价的范围内仍然具有解除或者变更义务人义务的权利，并持续至义务人收到权利已经转让、履行要向受让人给付的通知之时（而非之后）为止。

（2）只要被转让的权利以回报允诺的履行为条件的，即使存在转让通知，转让人和义务人依照合理的商业标准善意进行的任何合同变更或替代对受让人仍然有效。受让人获得变更后的合同或者替代合同项下的相应权利。

（3）即使受让人的权利存在瑕疵，但义务人在善意且不知道或没有理由知道该瑕疵的情况下给付了对价或者在其他方面改变了地位的，受让人仍然拥有转让人曾拥有的解除或者变更义务人义务的相同权利。

（4）有被公认是被转让权利的象征或者证明的书面文件的，解除或者变更对下列人员不生效力：

（a）所有人或者有撤销权的转让人，但书面文件由其给予，或者由占有书面文件的人给予且经其同意并存在必要的背书或者转让的除外；

（b）在善意且不知道或者没有理由知道解除或者变更存在的情况下，占有该书面文件且支付了对价的后续受让人。

§ 339. Protection of Obligor in Case of Adverse Claims

Where a claim adverse to that of an assignee subjects the obligor to a substantial risk beyond that imposed on him by his contract, the obligor will be granted such relief as is equitable in the circumstances.

第339条 存在对抗请求时对义务人的保护

与受让人的请求对抗的请求，将义务人置于超出合同向其施加的风险之外的实质性风险之中的，义务人将会获得具体情形下的公平救济。

TOPIC 5. PRIORITIES BETWEEN ASSIGNEE AND ADVERSE CLAIMANTS
第五节 受让人与对抗请求人之间的优先顺序

§ 340. Effect of Assignment on Priority and Security

（1）An assignee is entitled to priority of payment from the obligor's insolvent estate to the extent that the assignor would have been so entitled in the absence of assignment.

（2）Where an assignor holds collateral as security for the assigned right and does not effectively transfer the collateral to the assignee, the assignor is a constructive trustee of the collateral for the assignee in accordance with the rules stated for pledges in §§ 29-34 of the Restatement of Security.

第 340 条　转让对优先性[1]和担保的效力

（1）不发生转让时，转让人有从义务人不能抵债的财产中获得优先偿付的权利的，受让人在此范围内也具有优先受偿权。

（2）转让人持有被转让权利的担保物，但没有将担保物有效转让给受让人的，根据《担保法重述》第 29~34 条所述有关质物的规则，转让人是受让人的推定担保物受托人。

§ 341. Creditors of an Assignor

（1）Except as provided by statute, the right of an assignee is superior to a judicial lien subsequently obtained against the property of the assignor, unless the assignment is ineffective or revocable or is voidable by the assignor or by the person obtaining the lien or is in fraud of creditors.

---

〔1〕 优先性（priority），priority 尽管在本语境中也可以译为"优先权"，但为了与第 341 条中 lien 的译文相区分，故作此译。

（2）Notwithstanding the superiority of the right of an assignee, an obligor who does not receive notification of the assignment until after he has lost his opportunity to assert the assignment as a defense in the proceeding in which the judicial lien was obtained is discharged from his duty to the assignee to the extent of his satisfaction of the lien.

第 341 条　转让人的债权人

（1）除制定法另有规定的以外，受让人的权利优先于后续获得的针对转让人财产的司法优先权[1]，但转让不产生效力或者可撤销的，或者可以由转让人或者获得该优先权的人撤销的，或者欺诈债权人的除外。

（2）尽管受让人的权利具有优先性，但义务人失去了在产生司法优先权的程序中以权利转让作为抗辩的机会之后才收到转让通知的，义务人对受让人的义务在其清偿该优先权的范围之内解除。

§ 342. Successive Assignees from the Same Assignor

Except as otherwise provided by statute, the right of an assignee is superior to that of a subsequent assignee of the same right from the same assignor, unless

（a）the first assignment is ineffective or revocable or is voidable by the assignor or by the subsequent assignee; or

（b）the subsequent assignee in good faith and without knowledge or reason to know of the prior assignment gives value and obtains

 （i）payment or satisfaction of the obligation,

 （ii）judgment against the obligor,

 （iii）a new contract with the obligor by novation, or

 （iv）possession of a writing of a type customarily accepted as a symbol or as evidence of the right assigned.

---

〔1〕　司法优先权（judicial lien），即通过法律程序获得的优先权 Garner（2009：1008）。关于"lien"的理解，译者采用傅郁林（1999）的观点，认为内涵是大于"留置权"的"优先权"。参见傅郁林："法律术语的翻译与法律概念的解释——以海上货物留置权的翻译和解释为例"，载《北大法律评论》1999 年第 2 卷第 1 辑。Garner（2009：1006）也认为，"lien"不以债权人占有财产为要件。

第 342 条　同一转让人的多个受让人

若非制定法另有规定，受让人的权利优先于同一转让人转让同一权利的后续受让人，但下列情形除外：

（a）第一次转让不产生效力或者是可撤销的，或者可以由转让人或者由后续受让人撤销的；或者

（b）在善意且不知道或者没有理由知道先前转让的情况下，后续受让人提供了对价，并且获得了

（i）受偿或者债务清偿的，

（ii）针对义务人的判决的，

（iii）以更新形式与义务人缔结的新合同的，或者

（iv）通常被认为是被转让权利的象征或者证明的书面文件的占有的。

§ 343. Latent Equities

If an assignor's right against the obligor is held in trust or constructive trust for or subject to a right of avoidance or equitable lien of another than the obligor, an assignee does not so hold it if he gives value and becomes an assignee in good faith and without notice of the right of the other.

第 343 条　隐蔽的衡平请求权

转让人对义务人的权利是以信托或者推定信托的形式为义务人以外的他人持有的，或者受到义务人以外的他人的撤销权或者衡平优先权的限制的，如果受让人在善意且不知悉对方权利的情况下支付了对价并成为受让人，则不再以原有方式持有转让权利。

第十六章

救 济

Chapter 16
REMEDIES

TOPIC 1.　IN GENERAL
第一节　一般规则

§ 344. Purposes of Remedies

Judicial remedies under the rules stated in this Restatement serve to protect one or more of the following interests of a promisee：

(a) his "expectation interest", which is his interest in having the benefit of his bargain by being put in as good a position as he would have been in had the contract been performed,

(b) his "reliance interest", which is his interest in being reimbursed for loss caused by reliance on the contract by being put in as good a position as he would have been in had the contract not been made, or

(c) his "restitution interest", which is his interest in having restored to him any benefit that he has conferred on the other party.

第344条　救济的目的

根据本重述所述规则，司法救济旨在保护受诺人的下述一种或多种权益：

(a) 受诺人的"期待权益"，是指通过将受诺人置于合同得到履行时的相同地位，从而使其具有的取得交易利益的权益，

(b) 受诺人的"信赖权益"，是指通过将受诺人置于合同从未成立时的相同地位，从而使其具有的获得因信赖合同而造成的损失补偿的权益，或者

(c) 受诺人的"返还权益"，是指已经授予对方当事人的任何利益得以返还的权益。

§ 345. Judicial Remedies Available

The judicial remedies available for the protection of the interests stated in §344 include a judgment or order （a） awarding a sum of money due under the contract or as damages,

（b） requiring specific performance of a contract or enjoining its non-perform-ance,

（c） requiring restoration of a specific thing to prevent unjust enrichment,

（d） awarding a sum of money to prevent unjust enrichment,

（e） declaring the rights of the parties, and

（f） enforcing an arbitration award.

第 345 条　可以获取的司法救济

为保护第 344 条所述的权益，可以获取的司法救济包括以下判决或者命令：

（a） 判令支付合同到期金额，或者支付特定金额作为损害赔偿金，

（b） 要求具体履行合同，或者禁止合同的不履行，

（c） 要求返还特定之物以防不当得利，

（d） 判令支付特定数额以防不当得利，

（e） 宣布当事人的权利，以及

（f） 强制执行仲裁裁决。

TOPIC 2.　ENFORCEMENT BY AWARD OF DAMAGES
第二节　通过判令支付损害赔偿金强制执行合同

§ 346. Availability of Damages

（1） The injured party has a right to damages for any breach by a party against whom the contract is enforceable unless the claim for damages has been suspended or discharged.

（2） If the breach caused no loss or if the amount of the loss is not proved under the rules stated in this Chapter, a small sum fixed without regard to the amount of loss will be awarded as nominal damages.

第 346 条 损害赔偿金的获得

（1）合同当事人违约且合同可以对其强制执行的，受害人有权获得损害赔偿金，但损害赔偿请求已经被中止或者解除的除外。

（2）违约没有造成损失，或者损失数额无法依据本章所述规则得以证明的，判令支付与损失数额无关的较小数额作为名义损害赔偿金。

§ 347. Measure of Damages in General

Subject to the limitations stated in §§ 350-53, the injured party has a right to damages based on his expectation interest as measured by

(a) the loss in the value to him of the other party's performance caused by its failure or deficiency, plus

(b) any other loss, including incidental or consequential loss, caused by the breach, less

(c) any cost or other loss that he has avoided by not having to perform.

第 347 条 损害赔偿金计算的一般规则

在符合第 350~353 条所述规则限制的情况下，受害人有权取得基于其期待权益的损害赔偿金，计算方式为：

（a）因对方未履行或者履行存在瑕疵而导致其蒙受的履行价值的损失，加上

（b）违约造成的任何其他损失，包括附带的或者后果性的损失，减去

（c）受害人不必履行合同所避免的任何成本或者其他损失。

§ 348. Alternatives to Loss in Value of Performance

(1) If a breach delays the use of property and the loss in value to the injured party is not proved with reasonable certainty, he may recover damages based on the rental value of the property or on interest on the value of the property.

(2) If a breach results in defective or unfinished construction and the loss in value to the injured party is not proved with sufficient certainty, he may recover damages based on

（a） the diminution in the market price of the property caused by the breach, or

（b） the reasonable cost of completing performance or of remedying the defects if that cost is not clearly disproportionate to the probable loss in value to him.

（3） If a breach is of a promise conditioned on a fortuitous event and it is uncertain whether the event would have occurred had there been no breach, the injured party may recover damages based on the value of the conditional right at the time of breach.

第 348 条　履行价值损失的替代

（1） 违约造成财产使用的延误，且受害人的价值损失证明没有达到合理的确定性的，受害人可以基于财产的租赁价值或者财产价值的利息取得损害赔偿金。

（2） 违约导致有瑕疵或者未完工的建筑物，且受害人的价值损失证明没有达到充分的[1]确定性的，受害人损害赔偿金的取得可以：

（a） 基于违约造成的该财产市场价格的降低，或者

（b） 完成履行或者补救瑕疵产生的合理费用与受害人很可能产生的价值损失并非明显不成比例的，基于该合理费用。

（3） 违反了以偶发事件为条件的允诺，且即使没有违约也不确定该事件是否发生的，受害人可以基于违约时附条件权利的价值获得损害赔偿金。

§ 349. Damages Based On Reliance Interest

As an alternative to the measure of damages stated in § 347, the injured party has a right to damages based on his reliance interest, including expenditures made in preparation for performance or in performance, less any loss that the party in breach can prove with reasonable certainty the injured party would have suffered had the contract been performed.

第 349 条　基于信赖权益的损害赔偿金

作为第 347 条所述的损害赔偿金计算标准的替代，受害人有权基于信赖

---

〔1〕　充分的（sufficient），参见第 249 条注释 2。

权益取得损害赔偿金，包括准备履行或者履行过程中的费用支出，减去违约方能够以合理的确定性证明受害人在合同得以履行时也会蒙受的损失。

§ 350. Avoidability as a Limitation on Damages

（1）Except as stated in Subsection（2）, damages are not recoverable for loss that the injured party could have avoided without undue risk, burden, or humiliation.

（2）The injured party is not precluded from recovery by the rule stated in Subsection（1）to the extent that he has made reasonable but unsuccessful efforts to avoid loss.

第 350 条　可避免性对损害赔偿金的限制

（1）除第（2）款所述规则以外，受害人在不承担不当的风险、负担或耻辱的情况下本可以避免的损失，不能取得损害赔偿金。

（2）已经尽了合理努力但是未能成功避免损害发生的，受害人的赔偿在此范围内不因第（1）款所述规则而受阻却。

§ 351. Unforeseeability and Related Limitations on Damages

（1）Damages are not recoverable for loss that the party in breach did not have reason to foresee as a probable result of the breach when the contract was made.

（2）Loss may be foreseeable as a probable result of a breach because it follows from the breach

（a）in the ordinary course of events, or

（b）as a result of special circumstances, beyond the ordinary course of events, that the party in breach had reason to know.

（3）A court may limit damages for foreseeable loss by excluding recovery for loss of profits, by allowing recovery only for loss incurred in reliance, or otherwise if it concludes that in the circumstances justice so requires in order to avoid disproportionate compensation.

第 351 条　不可预见性以及有关因素对损害赔偿金的限制

（1）违约方订立合同时没有理由预见到会成为违约的高概率结果的损失，不能取得损害赔偿金。

（2）在下列情形下引起的违约损失，可能是可预见的违约高概率结果：

（a）在事物通常的发展过程中产生的，或者

（b）不是在事物的通常发展过程中产生，而是违约方有理由知道的特殊情形导致的。

（3）如果法院认为，在具体情形下，为了避免不相称的赔偿而为公正所需时，法院可以通过排除利润损失赔偿、只准予信赖损失赔偿或者采取其他方式对可预见性损失的赔偿进行限制。

§ 352. Uncertainty as a Limitation on Damages

Damages are not recoverable for loss beyond an amount that the evidence permits to be established with reasonable certainty.

第 352 条　不确定性对损害赔偿金的限制

超出证据所能证明的合理确定性范围的损失，不能取得损害赔偿金。

§ 353. Loss Due to Emotional Disturbance

Recovery for emotional disturbance will be excluded unless the breach also caused bodily harm or the contract or the breach is of such a kind that serious emotional disturbance was a particularly likely result.

第 353 条　精神伤害产生的损失

精神伤害不能获得赔偿，但违约同时造成了身体伤害，或者该类合同或该类违约尤其容易引起严重的精神伤害的除外。

§ 354. Interest as Damages

（1） If the breach consists of a failure to pay a definite sum in money or to render a performance with fixed or ascertainable monetary value, interest is recoverable from the time for performance on the amount due less all deductions to which the party in breach is entitled.

（2） In any other case, such interest may be allowed as justice requires on the amount that would have been just compensation had it been paid when performance was due.

第 354 条　利息作为损害赔偿金

（1）由于没有支付数额确定的金钱，或者没有给付具有确定或者可确定金钱价值的履行而违约的，根据应付数额减去违约方有权扣除的部分，自应予履行之时起计算并取得利息赔偿。

（2）在任何其他情况下，如果履行到期即行支付特定数额将能构成公平赔偿的，按照该数额并根据公正的要求计算并取得利息。

§ 355. Punitive Damages

Punitive damages are not recoverable for a breach of contract unless the conduct constituting the breach is also a tort for which punitive damages are recoverable.

第 355 条　惩罚性损害赔偿金

违反合同的，不能取得惩罚性损害赔偿金，但同时构成了应取得惩罚性损害赔偿金的侵权行为的除外。

§ 356. Liquidated Damages and Penalties

（1） Damages for breach by either party may be liquidated in the agreement but only at an amount that is reasonable in the light of the anticipated or actual loss caused by the breach and the difficulties of proof of loss. A term fixing unreasonably large liquidated damages is unenforceable on grounds of public policy as a penalty.

(2) A term in a bond providing for an amount of money as a penalty for non-occurrence of the condition of the bond is unenforceable on grounds of public policy to the extent that the amount exceeds the loss caused by such non-occurrence.

第356条　约定损害赔偿金与惩罚

(1) 任何一方当事人违约产生的赔偿金都可以在合同中约定，但只能是根据违约造成的预期损失或者现实损失以及损失证明的难度而确定的合理数额。合同条款规定了不合理的大额违约金的，是因违反公共政策而不可强制执行的惩罚性条款。

(2) 保函条款规定了保函条件不成就时作为惩罚的金钱数额的，在超出条件不成就造成的损失的范围内，因违反公共政策而不可强制执行。

TOPIC 3. ENFORCEMENT BY SPECIFIC PERFORMANCE AND INJUNCTION
第三节　通过具体履行和禁止令强制执行合同

§ 357. Availability of Specific Performance and Injunction

(1) Subject to the rules stated in §§ 359-69, specific performance of a contract duty will be granted in the discretion of the court against a party who has committed or is threatening to commit a breach of the duty.

(2) Subject to the rules stated in §§ 359-69, an injunction against breach of a contract duty will be granted in the discretion of the court against a party who has committed or is threatening to commit a breach of the duty if

(a) the duty is one of forbearance, or

(b) the duty is one of act and specific performance would be denied only for reasons that are inapplicable to an injunction.

第357条　具体履行与禁止令的获得

(1) 在符合第359~369条所述规则的前提下，法院裁量判予合同义务的具体履行，针对违反合同义务或者以违反合同义务相威胁的当事人实施。

（2）在符合第359~369条所述规则的前提下且有下列情形的，法院裁量判予违反合同义务的禁止令，针对违反合同义务或者以违反合同义务相威胁的当事人实施：

（a）合同义务属于不行为的，或者

（b）合同义务属于行为，且仅仅由于适用禁止令时不存在的障碍而无法适用具体履行的[1]。

§ 358. Form of Order and Other Relief

（1）An order of specific performance or an injunction will be so drawn as best to effectuate the purposes for which the contract was made and on such terms as justice requires. It need not be absolute in form and the performance that it requires need not be identical with that due under the contract.

（2）If specific performance or an injunction is denied as to part of the performance that is due, it may nevertheless be granted as to the remainder.

（3）In addition to specific performance or an injunction, damages and other relief may be awarded in the same proceeding and an indemnity against future harm may be required.

第358条　命令的方式及其他救济

（1）具体履行命令或者禁止令的签发，是为最大程度地实现合同订立的目的，并根据公正的要求适用于适宜的条款。命令的形式不必绝对，所要求的履行不必与合同规定的履行完全等同。

（2）具体履行或者禁止令针对部分到期履行被驳回的，仍然可以针对剩余到期履行适用。

（3）除具体履行或者禁止令以外，在同一诉讼程序中还可以判予损害赔偿金和其他救济，也可以为防止将来的损害而判令补偿。

---

[1]　按照原文视角翻译有些不好理解。本句的意思是：合同义务属于特定行为，法院本来可以发出具体履行命令，但是由于特定原因无法具体履行，而发出禁止令则不存在这些原因，因而法院可以发出禁止令，禁止从事与义务不相一致的行为，从而达到间接强制执行义务的目的。详见"重述"原文本条官方评论 b。

§ 359. Effect of Adequacy of Damages

(1) Specific performance or an injunction will not be ordered if damages would be adequate to protect the expectation interest of the injured party.

(2) The adequacy of the damage remedy for failure to render one part of the performance due does not preclude specific performance or injunction as to the contract as a whole.

(3) Specific performance or an injunction will not be refused merely because there is remedy for breach other than damages, but such a remedy may be considered in exercising discretion under the rule stated in §357.

第 359 条　充分的损害赔偿金的效力

(1) 损害赔偿金可以充分保护受害人的期待权益的，不再指令具体履行或者禁止令。

(2) 损害赔偿金针对未能给付到期履行的一部分是充分救济的，不阻却针对合同整体适用具体履行或者禁止令。

(3) 具体履行或者禁止令不会仅仅因为存在损害赔偿金之外的救济而被拒绝，但根据第 357 条所述规则进行裁量时，此救济可以纳入考量范围。

§ 360. Factors Affecting Adequacy of Damages

In determining whether the remedy in damages would be adequate, the following circumstances are significant:

(a) the difficulty of proving damages with reasonable certainty,

(b) the difficulty of procuring a suitable substitute performance by means of money awarded as damages, and

(c) the likelihood that an award of damages could not be collected.

第 360 条　损害赔偿金充分性的影响因素

确定损害赔偿金救济是否充分时，下列情形具有重要意义：

(a) 以合理的确定性证明获得损害赔偿金的难度，

（b）通过判予金钱形式的损害赔偿金能够获取适宜的替代履行的难度，以及

（c）所判予的损害赔偿金无法收取的可能性。

§ 361. Effect of Provision for Liquidated Damages

Specific performance or an injunction may be granted to enforce a duty even though there is a provision for liquidated damages for breach of that duty.

第 361 条　约定损害赔偿金的效力

即使合同约定了违反合同义务时的损害赔偿金条款，仍然可以准予具体履行或者以禁止令强制执行该合同义务。

§ 362. Effect of Uncertainty of Terms

Specific performance or an injunction will not be granted unless the terms of the contract are sufficiently certain to provide a basis for an appropriate order.

第 362 条　条款不确定的效力

除合同条款充分确定，能够构成签发适宜命令的基础以外，不准予具体履行或者发出禁止令。

§ 363. Effect of Insecurity as to the Agreed Exchange

Specific performance or an injunction may be refused if a substantial part of the agreed exchange for the performance to be compelled is unperformed and its perform-ance is not secured to the satisfaction of the court.

第 363 条　约定交换未经担保的效力

当事人要求强制履行时，履行对应的约定交换中的实质部分并没有履行，也没有提供法院所认可的履行担保的，具体履行或者禁止令可以拒绝。

§ 364. Effect of Unfairness

（1）Specific performance or an injunction will be refused if such relief would be

unfair because

(a) the contract was induced by mistake or by unfair practices, or

(b) the relief would cause unreasonable hardship or loss to the party in breach or to third persons, or

(c) the exchange is grossly inadequate or the terms of the contract are otherwise unfair.

(2) Specific performance or an injunction will be granted in spite of a term of the agreement if denial of such relief would be unfair because it would cause unreasonable hardship or loss to the party seeking relief or to third persons.

第 364 条　不公平的效力

(1) 具体履行或者禁止令由于下列原因会导致不公平的，该救济将被拒绝：

(a) 合同是错误的或者不公平的做法所诱使的结果的，或者

(b) 该救济会给违约方或者第三人造成不合理的困难或者损失的，或者

(c) 交换严重不对等，或者合同条款在其他方面是不公平的。

(2) 拒绝具体履行或者禁止令救济将会给寻求救济的当事人或者第三人造成不合理的困难或者损失，因而导致不公平的，即使存在不公平的协议条款[1]，也准予具体履行或者禁止令。

§ 365. Effect of Public Policy

Specific performance or an injunction will not be granted if the act or forbearance that would be compelled or the use of compulsion is contrary to public policy.

第 365 条　公共政策的效力

被强制执行的行为或者不行为，或者使用强制本身与公共政策相悖的，不判予具体履行或者禁止令。

---

〔1〕　即使存在不公平的协议条款（in spite of a term of the agreement），译者根据本条第（1）款（c）项以及"重述"原文本条评论 c 加译"不公平的"一词，尽管不加译会导致不可读，但加译毕竟带有阐释成分，是否正确，还请读者考证。

§ 366. Effect of Difficulty in Enforcement or Supervision

A promise will not be specifically enforced if the character and magnitude of the performance would impose on the court burdens in enforcement or supervision that are disproportionate to the advantages to be gained from enforcement and to the harm to be suffered from its denial.

第366条 强制执行或者监督困难的效力

履行的性质与重要性会给法院的强制执行或者监督造成负担，且与强制执行带来的好处以及与不予强制执行所产生的损害不成比例的，允诺不予具体强制执行。

§ 367. Contracts for Personal Service or Supervision

（1）A promise to render personal service will not be specifically enforced.

（2）A promise to render personal service exclusively for one employer will not be enforced by an injunction against serving another if its probable result will be to compel a performance involving personal relations the enforced continuance of which is undesirable or will be to leave the employee without other reasonable means of making a living.

第367条 提供个人服务或者监督的合同

（1）提供个人服务的允诺不予具体强制执行。

（2）对于专门为一个雇主提供个人服务的允诺，签发禁止令禁止为他人服务时，很可能会导致强迫涉及个人关系的履行，且强制这种个人关系的持续是不合适的，或者很可能会使受雇人再无其他合理谋生手段的，不以禁止令的形式强制执行。

§ 368. Effect of Power of Termination

（1）Specific performance or an injunction will not be granted against a party who can substantially nullify the effect of the order by exercising a power of termination or avoidance.

(2) Specific performance or an injunction will not be denied merely because the party seeking relief has a power to terminate or avoid his duty unless the power could be used, in spite of the order, to deprive the other party of reasonable security for the agreed exchange for his performance.

第 368 条　终止权的效力

(1) 当事人可以通过行使终止权或撤销权而实质性地导致法院的具体履行命令或者禁止令无效的，具体履行或者禁止令不适用于该当事人。

(2) 不仅仅因为寻求救济的当事人有权终止或者撤销自己的义务就不准予具体履行或者禁止令，但即使法院签发命令，该权利也可剥夺对方履行对应的约定交换的合理担保的除外。

§ 369. Effect of Breach by Party Seeking Relief

Specific performance or an injunction may be granted in spite of a breach by the party seeking relief, unless the breach is serious enough to discharge the other party's remaining duties of performance.

第 369 条　寻求救济的当事人违约的效力

即使寻求救济的当事人违约也可以准予具体履行或者禁止令，但违约的严重程度足以使对方剩余履行义务解除的除外。

TOPIC 4. RESTITUTION
第四节　返还

§ 370. Requirement That Benefit Be Conferred

A party is entitled to restitution under the rules stated in this Restatement only to the extent that he has conferred a benefit on the other party by way of part performance or reliance.

第 370 条　必须已经提供利益

只有在因部分履行或者信赖已经向对方提供利益的范围内，当事人才有权根据本重述所述规则获得返还。

§ 371. Measure of Restitution Interest

If a sum of money is awarded to protect a party's restitution interest, it may as justice requires be measured by either

(a) the reasonable value to the other party of what he received in terms of what it would have cost him to obtain it from a person in the claimant's position, or

(b) the extent to which the other party's property has been increased in value or his other interests advanced.

第 371 条　返还权益的计算

为保护当事人的返还权益而判予一定数额的金钱的，根据公正的要求采取下列方式之一计算：

(a) 对方当事人所获利益的合理数值，根据对方当事人从处在请求人位置的他人处获得相同利益所产生的支出确定；或者

(b) 对方当事人财产增值或者其他权益增加的幅度。

§ 372. Specific Restitution

(1) Specific restitution will be granted to a party who is entitled to restitution, except that:

(a) specific restitution based on a breach by the other party under the rule stated in § 373 may be refused in the discretion of the court if it would unduly interfere with the certainty of title to land or otherwise cause injustice, and

(b) specific restitution in favor of the party in breach under the rule stated in § 374 will not be granted.

(2) A decree of specific restitution may be made conditional on return of or compensation for anything that the party claiming restitution has received.

（3）If specific restitution, with or without a sum of money, will be substantially as effective as restitution in money in putting the party claiming restitution in the position he was in before rendering any performance, the other party can discharge his duty by tendering such restitution before suit is brought and keeping his tender good.

第 372 条　具体返还

（1）除下列情形以外，有权获得返还的当事人准予具体返还：

（a）第 373 条所述规则规定的基于对方当事人违约产生的具体返还，如果会对土地产权的确定性造成不当干预，或者在其他方面造成不公正的，法院可以裁量拒绝；以及

（b）第 374 条所述规则规定的有利于违约方的具体返还不予准许。

（2）具体返还判决的作出，可以以请求返还的当事人返还已获收益或者对此作出补偿为条件。

（3）具体返还无论是否伴有金钱给付，如果在使请求返还方恢复给付履行前的地位方面实质上与返还金钱同样有效的，对方当事人可以通过在起诉之前提交具体返还并保持提交有效而解除己方义务。

§ 373. Restitution When Other Party Is in Breach

（1）Subject to the rule stated in Subsection（2）, on a breach by non-performance that gives rise to a claim for damages for total breach or on a repudiation, the injured party is entitled to restitution for any benefit that he has conferred on the other party by way of part performance or reliance.

（2）The injured party has no right to restitution if he has performed all of his duties under the contract and no performance by the other party remains due other than payment of a definite sum of money for that performance.

第 373 条　他方当事人违约时的返还

（1）在符合本条第（2）款所述规则的情况下，不履行违约产生完全违约损害赔偿请求权的，或者存在拒绝履行的，受害人因部分履行或者信赖而给予对方当事人的任何利益有权获得返还。

（2）受害人已经履行了合同项下的所有义务，且对方当事人除了因该履行而应支付确定数额的金钱之外别无其他应履行义务的，受害人无权获得返还。

§ 374. Restitution in Favor of Party in Breach

（1）Subject to the rule stated in Subsection（2）, if a party justifiably refuses to perform on the ground that his remaining duties of performance have been discharged by the other party's breach, the party in breach is entitled to restitution for any benefit that he has conferred by way of part performance or reliance in excess of the loss that he has caused by his own breach.

（2）To the extent that, under the manifested assent of the parties, a party's performance is to be retained in the case of breach, that party is not entitled to restitution if the value of the performance as liquidated damages is reasonable in the light of the anticipated or actual loss caused by the breach and the difficulties of proof of loss.

第 374 条　有利于违约方的返还

（1）在符合本条第（2）款所述规则的情况下，一方当事人以其剩余履行义务因对方当事人违约而得以解除为由，合理地拒绝履行的，违约当事人对于因部分履行或者信赖而给予的利益中超过自己违约造成的损失的部分，有权获得返还。

（2）根据当事人各方的同意表示，一方当事人的履行在出现违约时应予保留的，如果根据违约所造成的预期或者现实损失以及证明损失的难度，将履行价值作为约定损害赔偿金是合理的，在此范围内该当事人无权获得返还。

§ 375. Restitution When Contract Is Within Statute of Frauds

A party who would otherwise have a claim in restitution under a contract is not barred from restitution for the reason that the contract is unenforceable by him because of the Statute of Frauds unless the Statute provides otherwise or its purpose would be frustrated by allowing restitution.

第375条　合同属于反欺诈法调整范围时的返还

当事人在其他方面都有合同项下的返还请求权的，不因反欺诈法的规定导致其不能强制执行合同而失去返还请求权，但反欺诈法另有规定，或者允许返还会导致反欺诈法目的落空的除外。

§ 376. Restitution When Contract Is Voidable

A party who has avoided a contract on the ground of lack of capacity, mistake, misrepresentation, duress, undue influence or abuse of a fiduciary relation is entitled to restitution for any benefit that he has conferred on the other party by way of part performance or reliance.

第376条　合同可撤销时的返还

当事人以缺乏行为能力、错误、误述、胁迫、不当影响或者滥用信托关系为由撤销合同的，其因部分履行或者信赖而给予对方当事人的任何利益有权得到返还。

§ 377. Restitution in Cases of Impracticability, Frustration, Non-Occurrence of Condition or Disclaimer by Beneficiary

A party whose duty of performance does not arise or is discharged as a result of impracticability of performance, frustration of purpose, non-occurrence of a condition or disclaimer by a beneficiary is entitled to restitution for any benefit that he has conferred on the other party by way of part performance or reliance.

第377条　履行不能、目的落空、条件不成就或者受益人弃权时的返还

当事人的履行义务因履行不能、目的落空、条件不成就或者受益人放弃权利而没有产生或者被解除的，其因部分履行或者信赖而给予对方当事人的任何利益有权获得返还。

TOPIC 5.　PRECLUSION BY ELECTION AND AFFIRMANCE
第五节　选择与确认产生阻却

§ 378. Election Among Remedies

If a party has more than one remedy under the rules stated in this Chapter, his manifestation of a choice of one of them by bringing suit or otherwise is not a bar to another remedy unless the remedies are inconsistent and the other party materially changes his position in reliance on the manifestation.

第378条　选择救济手段

根据本章所述规则，当事人有一种以上救济方式的，通过起诉或者其他方式作出选择其一的表示并不阻却其他的救济，但救济方式存在矛盾，且对方当事人因信赖该表示而实质性改变地位的除外。

§ 379. Election to Treat Duties of Performance Under Aleatory Contract As Discharged

If a right or duty of the injured party is conditional on an event that is fortuitous or is supposed by the parties to be fortuitous, he cannot treat his remaining duties to render performance as discharged on the ground of the other party's breach by non-performance if he does not manifest to the other party his intention to do so before any adverse change in the situation of the injured party resulting from the occurrence of that event or a material change in the probability of its occurrence.

第379条　选择将射幸合同项下的履行义务视为解除

受害人的权利或者义务以某一偶然事件的发生为条件，或者以当事人都认为具有偶然性质的事件的发生为条件的，如果受害人在事件发生或者发生概率产生重大改变引起受害人情况发生了不利变化之前，没有向对方当事人作出意思表示，说明将以对方不履行违约为由将自己剩余的给付履行义务视为解除的，则不能以此为由将自己的剩余给付履行义务视为解除。

§ 380. Loss of Power of Avoidance by Affirmance

(1) The power of a party to avoid a contract for incapacity, duress, undue influence or abuse of a fiduciary relation is lost if, after the circumstances that made the contract voidable have ceased to exist, he manifests to the other party his intention to affirm it or acts with respect to anything that he has received in a manner inconsistent with disaffirmance.

(2) The power of a party to avoid a contract for mistake or misrepresentation is lost if after he knows or has reason to know of the mistake or of the misrepresentation if it is non-fraudulent or knows of the misrepresentation if it is fraudulent, he manifests to the other party his intention to affirm it or acts with respect to anything that he has received in a manner inconsistent with disaffirmance.

(3) If the other party rejects an offer by the party seeking avoidance to return what he has received, the party seeking avoidance if entitled to restitution can, after the lapse of a reasonable time, enforce a lien on what he has received by selling it and crediting the proceeds toward his claim in restitution.

第 380 条　因确认而丧失撤销权

（1）使合同可撤销的缺乏行为能力、胁迫、不当影响或者滥用信托关系的情形消失之后，有权撤销合同的当事人向对方当事人作出确认的意思表示的，或者针对所收到的给付作出与不予确认不一致的行为的，当事人的撤销权消灭。

（2）当事人知道或者有理由知道存在错误或者非欺诈性误述之后，或者知道存在欺诈性误述之后，向对方当事人作出确认的意思表示，或者针对任何所收之物作出与不予承认不一致的行为的，因错误或者误述产生的合同撤销权消灭。

（3）对方当事人拒绝寻求撤销合同的当事人归还所收之物的提议的，寻求撤销合同的当事人如果有权取得返还，则可以在一段合理时间之后，通过将所收之物变卖、保存所得以供返还请求之用的方式，对所收之物行使优先权。

§ 381. Loss of Power of Avoidance by Delay

（1）The power of a party to avoid a contract for incapacity, duress, undue influence or abuse of a fiduciary relation is lost if, after the circumstances that made it voidable have ceased to exist, he does not within a reasonable time manifest to the other party his intention to avoid it.

（2）The power of a party to avoid a contract for misrepresentation or mistake is lost if after he knows of a fraudulent misrepresentation or knows or has reason to know of a non-fraudulent misrepresentation or mistake he does not within a reasonable time manifest to the other party his intention to avoid it. The power of a party to avoid a contract for non-fraudulent misrepresentation or mistake is also lost if the contract has been so far performed or the circumstances have otherwise so changed that avoidance would be inequitable and if damages will be adequate compensation.

（3）In determining what is a reasonable time, the following circumstances are significant:

（a）the extent to which the delay enabled or might have enabled the party with the power of avoidance to speculate at the other party's risk;

（b）the extent to which the delay resulted or might have resulted in justifiable reliance by the other party or by third persons;

（c）the extent to which the ground for avoidance was the result of any fault by either party; and

（d）the extent to which the other party's conduct contributed to the delay.

（4）If a right or duty of the party who has the power of avoidance for non-fraudulent misrepresentation or mistake is conditional on an event that is fortuitous or is supposed by the parties to be fortuitous, a manifestation of intention under Subsection（1）or（2）is not effective unless it is made before any adverse change in his situation resulting from the occurrence of that event or a material change in the probability of its occurrence.

第 381 条 因迟延而失去撤销权

（1）使得合同可撤销的缺乏行为能力、胁迫、不当影响或者滥用信托关系的情形消失之后，有权撤销合同的当事人没有在合理时间之内向对方当事人作出撤销合同的意思表示的，撤销权消灭。

（2）当事人知道存在欺诈性误述之后，或者知道或有理由知道存在非欺诈性误述或者错误之后，没有在合理时间之内向对方当事人作出撤销合同的意思表示的，因误述或者错误产生的合同撤销权消灭。合同已经履行的程度或者其他方面的情形变化会使得撤销合同不公平的，且损害赔偿金可以构成充分补偿的，因非欺诈性误述或者错误产生的撤销权也得以消灭。

（3）对于合理时间的确定，下列情形具有重要意义：

（a）迟延在何种程度上使得或者可能使得撤销权人利用了对方的风险；

（b）迟延在何种程度上令对方当事人或者第三人产生或者可能产生了合理信赖；

（c）撤销的理由在何种程度上是任一当事人过错的结果；以及

（d）对方当事人的行为在何种程度上造成了迟延。

（4）有权以非欺诈性误述或者错误为由撤销合同的当事人，如果其权利或者义务是以某一偶然事件的发生为条件，或者以当事人都认为具有偶然性质的事件的发生为条件的，第（1）款或者第（2）款规定的意思表示并不生效，但在事件发生或者发生概率产生重大改变，引起撤销权人情况发生不利变化之前作出的除外。

§ 382. Loss of Power to Affirm by Prior Avoidance

（1）If a party has effectively exercised his power of avoidance, a subsequent manifestation of intent to affirm is inoperative unless the other party manifests his assent to affirmance by refusal to accept a return of his performance or otherwise.

（2）A party has not exercised his power of avoidance under the rule stated in Subsection（1）until

（a）he has regained all or a substantial part of what he would be entitled to by way of restitution on avoidance,

（b）he has obtained a final judgment of or based on avoidance, or

（c）the other party has materially relied on or manifested his assent to a statement of disaffirmance.

第382条　因先前的撤销丧失确认权

（1）当事人有效行使撤销权后作出的确认意思表示无效，但对方当事人通过拒绝接受归还的履行或者以其他方式对确认表示同意的除外。

（2）只有在下列情形下，当事人才是根据第（1）款所述规则行使了撤销权：

（a）已经全部或者实质性地全部重新获得了撤销合同时有权取得返还之物的，

（b）已经获得了撤销合同的或者以撤销合同为基础的最终判决的，或者

（c）对方当事人已经对不予确认的陈述产生了实质性信赖或者作出了同意表示的。

§ 383. Avoidance in Part

A contract cannot be avoided in part except that where one or more corresponding pairs of part performances have been fully performed by one or both parties the rest of the contract can be avoided.

第383条　部分撤销

合同不得部分撤销，但一个或者一个以上的部分履行组合已经由一方或者双方当事人完全履行的，合同剩余部分可以撤销。

§ 384. Requirement That Party Seeking Restitution Return Benefit

（1）Except as stated in Subsection（2）, a party will not be granted restitution unless

（a）he returns or offers to return, conditional on restitution, any interest in property that he has received in exchange in substantially as good condition as when it was received by him, or

（b）the court can assure such return in connection with the relief granted.

（2）The requirement stated in Subsection（1）does not apply to property

（a）that was worthless when received or that has been destroyed or lost by the other party or as a result of its own defects,

(b) that either could not from the time of receipt have been returned or has been used or disposed of without knowledge of the grounds for restitution if justice requires that compensation be accepted in its place and the payment of such compensation can be assured, or

(c) as to which the contract apportions the price if that part of the price is not included in the claim for restitution.

第 384 条 寻求返还的当事人归还利益的要求

(1) 除第（2）款所述规则以外，当事人只有在下列情形下才会准予返还：

(a) 以返还为条件，归还或者提出归还作为交换收到的财产权益，且与收到之时实质上处于同样的良好状况的，或者

(b) 法院能够确保与准予的救济相关的此类归还的。

(2) 第（1）款所述要求不适用于下列财产：

(a) 收到时毫无价值的，或者被对方当事人毁坏或者丢失，或者由于本身瑕疵而毁坏或丢失的，

(b) 自收到之时起就无法归还，或者在不知道存在返还原因的情况下已经被使用或者被处理，且公平原则要求以补偿取代返还，补偿的给付也能够确保的，或者

(c) 价款在合同中进行了分割，该部分价款没有包含在返还请求之中的。

§ 385. Effect of Power of Avoidance on Duty of Performance or on Duty Arising Out of Breach

(1) Unless an offer to restore performance received is a condition of avoidance, a party has no duty of performance while his power of avoidance exists.

(2) If an offer to restore performance received is a condition of avoidance, a duty to pay damages is terminated by such an offer made before the power of avoidance is lost.

第385条　撤销权对履行义务或者对违约产生的义务的效力

（1）除提出归还收到的履行是撤销的条件以外，当事人在撤销权存续期间没有履行义务。

（2）提出归还收到的履行是撤销的条件的，在撤销权消灭之前提出归还时，支付损害赔偿金的义务终止。

译后记

美国合同法是判例法。关于合同法的判例浩如烟海，令学子望而生畏，而背后的一些原则又经常互相矛盾，让初学者感到无所适从。1923年美国法学会成立以后，致力于将乱麻般的判例规则归纳梳理，并以制定法的形式叙述成文，是为合同法"重述"。

"重述"虽非立法机关的产物，但其权威性与重要性却广为认可：两次《美国合同法重述》和《统一商法典》被一些法学家认为是二十世纪合同法领域的三大里程碑，"承载和代表了当今世界主流契约法理论思想：新古典契约法理论"，[1]而且美国法院判决时常援引，合同法著述几乎逢论必提，同时也是国内合同法领域的必读文献，是研究人员、涉外律师、法科学生快速了解美国合同法的最佳途径，是法律英语学习与研究的重要语料。

迄今，美国合同法共历经两次重述，本书原作即为"重述"当前的最新版本。本版共分十六章三百八十五条，每条包括规则、评论（内含"例示"）、重述注释等内容，行文简明扼要，释评精当贴切，内容权威丰富。译者本欲推出"重述"全译本，无奈作品篇幅宏大，原团队成员教学、科研任务繁重，无法确保翻译进程，只好先将规则部分译出，待时机成熟时再译介全文。

本译文附有英文原文，供读者比照阅读，这不仅可以督促译者勉力剖章析句、精心传译，以减少甚或消除译文可能产生的误导，还可以为读者提供很好的法律英语学习材料。

立法英语句式繁复，又有中英双语思维、文化的差异，使用汉语精确表

---

〔1〕 参见刘承韪：《英美契约法的变迁与发展》，北京大学出版社2014年版，第148页。

达原意并非易事。不少句子读来易懂，但形诸纸面文字却难，可谓"此中有真意，欲辨却无言"！面对此类问题，译者勉力居中"圆满调和"，在忠实原文的前提下，选词造句以汉语规范为规为矩，并谨守汉语言简意赅的传统，一稿译毕，必定反复阅读，删除一切可删之字，同时采用"厚译"策略，译语确实难解或者过于繁复时，或者因双语文化差异可能引起歧义时，便添加注释进行说明（但尽量避免评论性注释）。此外，中英术语若无等值的现成组合，则优先采用直译处理，同时加注说明。

为了保证理解和表述的正确，译者查阅了有关国内外立法、国际条约以及《美国合同法重述》第二版原书的"评论"与"例示"部分，也参阅了有关学术专著、文章和辞书，后者主要包括：

Brady, James B. Law, Language and Logic：the Legal Philosophy of Wesley Newcomb Hohfeld ［J］. *Transactions of the Charles S. Peirce Society*. 1972 (4).

Garner, Bryan A. *Black's Law Dictionary* ［Z］. West Publishing Co., 2009.

Farnsworth, E. Allan. *Farnsworth on Contracts* ［M］. Aspen Publishers, 2004.

薛波. 元照英美法词典 ［Z］. 北京：法律出版社，2003.

傅郁林. 法律术语的翻译与法律概念的解释——以海上货物留置权的翻译和解释为例 ［J］. 北大法律评论，1999 年第 2 卷第 1 辑.

林穗芳. 标点符号学习与应用 ［M］. 北京：人民出版社，2000.

刘承韪. 英美契约法的变迁与发展 ［M］. 北京：北京大学出版社，2014.

张法连. 英美法律术语辞典（英汉双解）［Z］. 上海：上海外语教育出版社，2014.

斯普兰克林. 美国财产法精解 ［M］. 钟书峰，译. 北京：北京大学出版社，2009.

杨桢. 英美契约法论 ［M］. 北京：北京大学出版社，2000.

王军. 美国合同法 ［M］. 北京：中国政法大学出版社，1996.

夏勇. 权利哲学的基本问题 ［J］. 法学研究，2004 (3).

译者谨对有关著述的作者表示感谢，同时也感谢美国法学会的翻译授权，感谢美国法学会版权经理 Nina Amster 女士为本项目的付出。中国人民大学杨敏教授十分关心项目进展，多次指导、帮助、鼓励，译者深为感激。河北师范大学顾维忧教授热心提供参考资料，译者甚为感谢。

中国政法大学外国语学院张法连教授担任本书译审，张法连教授工作繁忙，但仍然关心着本项目的方方面面并悉心指导。复旦大学法学院高凌云教授在美国讲学期间仍然拨冗为译者答疑解惑。两位教授的意见高屋建瓴、切中肯綮，使译者体会到了柳暗花明的愉悦。

翻译《美国合同法重述》是译者多年的梦想，但一朝梦想成真，欣喜之余却又惴惴不安：译文虽经数易其稿，但因译者水平所限，又加时间仓促，尚有不尽如人意之处，请方家不吝赐教，并将高论发至 devinlaw@ ruc. edu. cn。一字亦师，译者不胜感激。

暑去寒来，岁末已至，难忘戊戌日月。

徐文彬

2018 年 12 月 22 日于灵山湾畔

中国法律英语教学与测试研究会

China Association for Legal English Teaching and Testing

简　介

　　中国法律英语教学与测试研究会是由从事法律英语教学与测试研究的人员自愿组织起来的全国性民间学术团体，是中国专门用途英语教学研究会的专业学会，接受中国专门用途英语教学研究会和社团登记管理机关的业务指导和监督管理，独立运作。本会致力于促进法律英语教学与测试的研究，促进理论与实践相结合，促进法律英语新兴交叉学科增长点的培育，为国家外语能力的提升和培养国家战略所需的法律英语人才做出贡献。

　　本会的业务范围包括：（1）法律英语教学与测试的理论及应用研究；（2）与之相关的法律语言研究及法律领域内与英语能力有关的研究；（3）学会年会、学术研讨会、师资研修班等学术交流；（4）与实践部门合作进行的研究成果转化与推广工作；（5）法律英语培训与法律英语能力认证工作；（6）会刊创办及交流促进；（7）面向社会各界的咨询服务；（8）相关学术书刊、统编教材及音像制品的编辑出版；（9）有利于法律英语教学与法律英语人才培养的其他工作。

　　本会组织机构主要包括：（1）会员代表大会；（2）理事会；（3）常务理事会；（4）会长；（5）副会长；（6）秘书处。本会设有法律翻译专业委员会、法律英语证书考试专业委员会、英美法专业委员会以及语料库专业委员会，并已经在山东省和江苏省分别设立了分会。

本会已经多年连续开展学术活动，进行了一系列卓有成效的学术交流，取得了具有标志意义的成果，如：（1）成功召开了八届中国法律英语教学与测试国际研讨会，搭建了国内外法律英语专家学者广泛参与和深入交流的平台；（2）连续举办了多期"全国高等院校法律英语教师高级研修班"和"大学法律英语课程设计与教学方法研修班"，对高等学校教师实现转型和发展起到有力的促进作用；（3）组织开展了每年两次的法律英语证书（LEC）全国统一考试；（4）组织编写了一系列对法律英语语言研究、法律英语教学与测试研究、法律英语人才培养和法律英语教师发展有重要教学价值和学术价值的专著、辞书、教材等。

法律英语证书（LEC）考试简介

　　十八届四中全会明确提出加强涉外法治建设。2019 年 2 月 25 日习近平总书记在中央全面依法治国委员会第二次会议的重要讲话指出，要加快推进我国法域外适用的法律体系建设，加强涉外法治专业人才培养。然而，涉外法治人才严重短缺是我们必须面对的严峻现实。

　　涉外法治人才的培养是系统工程，不能一蹴而就，而应该立足长远，找准切入点。实际上，涉外法律工作的核心内容是英美法体系。有着上千年历史的英美法今天仍被广泛应用于美、英及加拿大等英联邦国家及地区。目前，联合国国际法院运用的司法程序依据英美法，国际贸易的基本规则同样依照英美法。英美法是我国法域外适用的法律体系建设的核心内容。近四十年来，我国的英美法教育一直被冷落，直至加入 WTO 后，我们才发现问题的严重性。英美法的载体就是法律英语，学好法律英语就能学好英美法，学习英美法也是学习法律英语的唯一正途。因而，就我国的高等教育现状而言，培养涉外法治人才最好的切入点就是法律英语。

　　由于法律英语的特殊性，国内一直没有一个科学的考核指标衡量法律从业人员专业英语的掌握程度。法律英语证书（Legal English Certificate，LEC）全国统一考试的推出填补了国内相关领域的空白。

　　法律英语证书（LEC）全国统一考试指导委员会依托中国政法大学和北京外国语大学具体组织考试工作，旨在为从事涉外业务的企业、律师事务所提供招募国际性人才的客观标准，同时督促国内法律从业人员提高专业英语水平。

　　法律英语证书（LEC）考试的题型、考察内容与美国的律师资格考试相近，同时又突出了法律英语语言运用的特色，并结合中国的实际增加了法律英语翻译测试。公检法机关和企事业单位从事涉外法务的工作人员；从事涉外法务的律师，公司法律部门的从业人员；高等院校法律、英语、经贸等专业的学生；愿意从事法律英语教学的教师以及社会上一切法律英语爱好者均可参加法律英语证书（LEC）考试。该考试证书是从事涉外法律服务工作人员专业英语水平的权威证明，通过考试并取得 LEC 也是赴美攻读法学专业及取得美国律师职业资格的可靠保证。

法律英语证书（LEC）考试每年举行两次，分别在 5 月份和 11 月份的最后一个周六举行，目前已在北京、上海、广州、重庆、杭州、济南、武汉、西安、保定、株洲、南宁、南京、厦门、甘肃、大连、青岛、郑州等城市设考点，法律英语证书（LEC）全国统一考试指导委员会全面负责组考工作。考试不受年龄、性别、职业、地区、学历等限制，持本人有效身份证件即可报名参加考试。

图书在版编目（ＣＩＰ）数据

美国合同法重述:第二版. 规则部分：汉、英/美国法学会编写；徐文彬译.—北京：
中国政法大学出版社,2022.12
书名原文：Restatement of the Law Second, Contracts
ISBN 978-7-5764-0345-9

Ⅰ.①美⋯　Ⅱ.①美⋯　②徐⋯　Ⅲ.①合同法－美国－汉、英　Ⅳ.①D971.23

中国版本图书馆CIP数据核字(2022)第029884号

美国合同法重述第二版·规则部分

书　名　MEIGUO HETONGFA CHONGSHU DIERBAN·GUIZE
　　　　BUFEN

出版者　中国政法大学出版社

地　址　北京市海淀区西土城路 25 号

邮　箱　fadapress@163.com

网　址　http://www.cuplpress.com (网络实名：中国政法大学出版社)

电　话　010-58908466(第七编辑部) 010-58908334(邮购部)

承　印　固安华明印业有限公司

开　本　720mm×960mm　1/16

印　张　16.5

字　数　260 千字

版　次　2022 年 12 月第 1 版

印　次　2022 年 12 月第 1 次印刷

定　价　88.00 元